CREATING IN CLOTH

Everyone can learn to create in cloth.

banners
wall hangings
stuffed toys
quilts
gifts

CREATING IN CLOTH

judith schoener kalina

CHRISTIAN HERALD BOOKS
Chappaqua, New York 10514

Photo credits: Pages 10 and 95 by Carolyn Fabricant and page 86 by Bill Lyons. All other photos and drawings
by the author, except for the works of Sharon McKain, Sister Helena Steffens-Meier, Virginia Churchill Bath,
Anders Holmquist, Sas Colby, and Liese Bronfenbrenner.

Dedication

This book is dedicated to my husband David and to our daughters Jenny and Nora, whose love and support have carried me through this project.

This book is also dedicated to the memory of my father-in-law, the Honorable Abraham I. Kalina, Justice of the Supreme Court of the State of New York, who would have been extremely proud to have seen its completion.

ACKNOWLEDGEMENTS

If there is a way to create a book alone, I do not know it. Special thanks go to my friend and typist Beeby Harold, who was wonderfully cheerful, helpful and supportive at all times. Love and thanks go to my husband David, who spent many hours editing the original manuscript. Grateful acknowledgement goes to my editor Judith Dykema, who maintained confidence throughout the development of this book, and to art director Dominick Cirri, who encouraged me with my drawings and designed this book. My thanks also to Gladys Boalt who gave helpful criticism and arranged for me to photograph the resources in the quilting chapter. Thanks go to the artists and craftspeople who willingly sent reproductions of their work, thus immensely enriching the book.

There are others who, while they did not take an active part in the development of this book, have so influenced and enriched the field of creating in cloth, that it would be remiss of me not to give them thankful mention: Jean Ray Laury, Norman LaLiberte, Lenore Davis, Sas Colby, and Rachel Maines.

CREATING IN CLOTH

JUNGLE, wall hanging by the author. This piece was made for a child's room. The long threads were not clipped to give a casual look and to encourage touching.

INTRODUCTION

Once people worked from dawn to dusk for food, clothing and shelter. There was little time for personal adornment, for refinement, for the decoration and creation of beautiful things. Yet there was a need for artistic expression and it found its way into all kinds of utilitarian objects.

Today, machines have taken over the making of things. We are surrounded with objects which are of plastic or other synthetic materials. While we may find these to be attractive, we still desire something truly beautiful: something homey, something handmade, not quite perfect nor stamped from a mold, but direct and spontaneous enough to remind us of its roots and our own. For there remains in each of us a need to express our visions, our ideas, our interests. A handmade object which we have created tells who we are and what we are thinking and feeling. It is a repository for memories.

Working with fabric is one mode of expression. From banners and quilts to stuffed dolls and toys, it has always been a true folk art. It began with the same needs for personal expression and adornment that we feel today. It was not sufficient to have a coat to keep out the chill; fine stitches and patterns were added. To have a padded blanket was not enough. It had to be beautifully quilted and decorated so that one could enjoy looking at it as well as sleeping under it.

Stitchery has never been rigid. Patterns were copied, but variations were made, combining the practical workaday world with personal expression. Quilters could reproduce the infinite variety of old patterns, but they also quickly chose to express their own lives through depicting social, political and religious events.

As a teacher, I have found that people of all ages and all levels of ability enjoy creating in cloth. The homemaker, the group leader and the child, in school, community or church—all find working with fabric rewarding and simple. Younger children enjoy quickly finished projects; older children can do elaborate and detailed work. The homemaker will find that it fits into family life. For example, I find that ideas come to me during walks with the family or when we go to the ballet, circus and museums. While I cook with my two daughters or read stories to them, I am still able to think about new projects. While I work my children can be around me; I can stitch, stuff and quilt while they work nearby, cutting, pinning and stitching or gluing their own little fabric pieces.

1

The author and her children working together.

But stitchery is not just for the individual. Groups are eager to experiment with fabric. Children and adults delight in something other than crayons and paints. They love the richness and variety and inexpensiveness of fabric. The world is filled with things to collect and glue or sew. There are trimmings, buttons, bells, stones, pieces of wood . . . the only limit here is range of imagination. I have taught stitchery to groups of adults and children ranging from the gifted to those with mental and physical handicaps and all have found value in the experience. Church and community groups too are finding that special communication and satisfaction comes from joining together to make quilts, wall hangings and banners on religious and other themes.

Beginning a project is the most difficult part. There is often the temptation to run to the store for a pre-stamped pattern. But after you have thought out what you want to do and overcome temporary qualms, you will find great pleasure in doing the entire project by yourself or with your group.

This book shows you how to begin, how to find and develop ideas, and how to translate them into a finished piece of work. The first section of this book concentrates on what goes into the making of the work: ideas, designs, color, materials and techniques; the last half takes projects through to completion: banners and wall hangings, quilts, dolls, stuffed toys and gifts.

This is a book of beginnings and of some endings. As you proceed through it, I hope you will begin to choose your own direction, freely accepting or discarding my ideas. The best will be your own creating in cloth.

—Judith Schoener Kalina

2

1. Getting Ideas

MY GRANDFATHER APPEARS TO ME IN A DREAM, wall hanging by the author.
Courtesy of Sylvia Feldshuh.

Getting Ideas

For something to have great value for me, I must discover it myself. I suspect it is the same with other people. A person, a place, an emotion cannot be fully known until personally experienced. We all can appreciate what someone else has to say, but if we are going to understand it completely, we must experience and express our understandings in our own ways.

The same is true of stitchery. You must choose what you are really interested in and what you want to create. One person loves birds, while another prefers butterflies. I love circuses, folk tales, fairy tales, and Bible stories. My work shows the subjects I favor. In one of my wall hangings, I intertwined my love for my grandfather with my love of folk tales. I knew my grandfather only when I was a small girl, when he sang songs, told tales and played games he had learned in his small and lively European village.

Your interests can be a starting point. You

CREATING IN CLOTH

need no exotic landscape, for even those at home or limited to a particular locale have rich resources. The great artists knew this. Rembrandt painted biblical events, but he peopled them with the humble men and women he found on Amsterdam's streets. Van Gogh painted the common sunflowers. Rousseau never left France, but he painted his dreams of faraway, exotic places. And Chagall painted the simple folk legends of his childhood. Your own house and backyard, people you meet, and stories you read are potential sources of inspiration.

Perhaps you are a young mother at home. Look around you. What do you see? Do you see children? Do they interest you? Make sketches or cut shapes from paper or cloth of their faces, their feet, their hands, and the things they enjoy. Work quickly without worrying whether they are exact. Try to simplify the outlines. Remember that fiber art is not based on the exact. It is a spontaneous and joyful art form.

You may be the person who loves birds; then respond to them in the way a child does. Look at birds, sketch them, try to under-

stand what makes them birds and gives them their "birdness." Read about birds. Find both realistic and abstract drawings and paintings of birds. Do some sketches. Immerse yourself in the subject of birds.

Go out to your garden or to one of your indoor plants and look at it with care. Lie down next to a rose bush or a tomato plant. Study it, smell it, feel it. Look at the insects, the rocks and all natural forms with the same intensity. But don't copy slavishly; simplify to basic lines and work quickly.

7

CREATING IN CLOTH

Watching your children create art can show you another way of seeing. A child perceives in a way we have forgotten. To a young child the sky is a ceiling, the sun falls over the edge of the earth, a table in front of a person means the body is cut off.

In their spontaneity, youngsters get at the essence of things. They seem to simplify and exaggerate in order to express themselves. There is an honesty to their work.

It is not a good idea to copy children's work because it is based upon their way of seeing as well as on their physical movements. But you can learn much from the work of children. I have made collages with my daughters and in seeing the way they work, with confidence and directness, I have learned to work that way too. In seeing their simplicity, I have learned to use simplicity as well as elaboration. In seeing their economy, how one line can describe a universe, I have learned to be economical. Their spontaneity and joy, their indulgence in the art experience for its own sake, for the sake of manipulating materials, for the sake of freedom and movement, have inspired a new freedom and joy in my own work.

ANGEL PRINCESS, drawing by Nora Kalina at age six.

If you do not have the opportunity to observe children, perhaps there is something about your home that you especially enjoy. What interests you most? Is it an area, a particular room, a treasured object? Is it the sun glinting through the window, a plant in luxuriant bloom? Admirers of Matisse love finding his favorite belongings in picture after picture. You, too, can show your feelings about your home.

CREATING IN CLOTH

PATRIARCH (IN A BROWN ROBE), quilted batik wall hanging by Morag Benepe. From the collection of Barbara Tetteh-Larty.

Or consider stories or books. When you read, do you have a vision of how things should look? When you read the story of Jonah, how do you see Jonah? What does his face look like? What kind of expression does he have? What are his surroundings like? What colors fit his story?

Try enlarging or diminishing a detail or an area. Choose interpretive colors and decide what adds meaning to the subject.

If you enjoy geometric or abstract shapes, you need only your personal response to forms and colors. You might like to experiment with paper weaving.

Detail from A BIRTHDAY QUILT, designed by Gladys Boalt and executed by Lorraine Cheney.

For ideas, save pictures that attract you. Often someone else's work may be merely a link to your own experiences. This person's illustration of a holiday celebration may remind you of celebrations at home. That person's view of a childhood landscape may remind you of the place you knew as a child. Think of these illustrations as a source of reference. Find out what has inspired and attracted you. Dwell on that part; expand it.

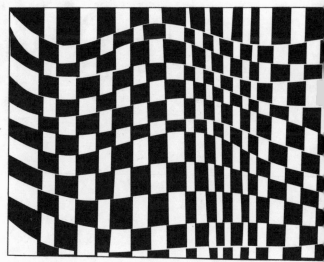

CREATING IN CLOTH

Or cutting, in a way similar to cutting paper dolls. Or discovering what happens when you explode a shape as in the fish shape below.

Sometimes ideas come from working with textures and patterns. Collect pieces of materials, the smooth and the rough, the close or loosely woven. In the same way you

have been mixing upholstery, drapery fabrics, and wallpaper in your home, experiment with different patterns in cloth. Nature is a wonderful resource for textures and patterns. Look at the various leaf patterns. Notice the variety, but also the repetition.

During this early time enjoy the luxury of discovery. Absorbing your surroundings, experimenting with sizes and shapes, immersing yourself in ideas—all this "play" is a cru-

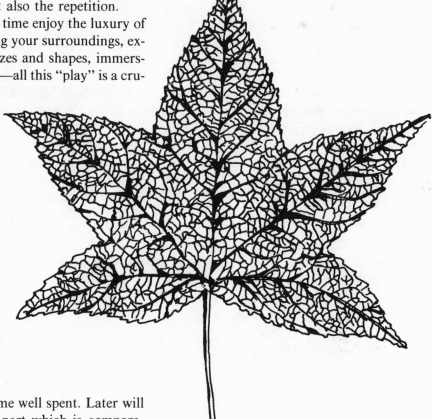

cial first step and time well spent. Later will come the technical part which is comparatively easy. Techniques come as you need them and skills improve as you use them. But now is the time you must say, "I like this. I am going to try this. I am going to have faith in my own ideas."

Some fear the word *creativity,* because they think it demands a special kind of talent. But creativity begins in a small way and builds on what has gone before. I have heard the same folk tune sung in different ways, sometimes with only a slight variation, sometimes with great differences. One fairy tale can have endless versions, some making it unrecognizable, others making it only slightly different from the "original." All of these changes had a beginning, something to lean on, to draw from. This musician added a little bit of special finger work; that story teller added a bit of local color. The personal stamp of uniqueness can be added to everything you do, too. Remember how you gave a child pleasure when you put him or her into a familiar story, when he or she became the hero? Your own pleasure will be a like one, when each piece you make will be a way of expressing yourself.

You will find that as you begin working, one notion will lead to another, sometimes even to another piece of work. Work on several at the same time, as I do, or file your ideas for a later time. While you plan your designs you will need several hours of quiet for concentration away from your family. You may want to refer to the second chapter on design at this point, or you might turn to the last half of the book to begin on an individual project. After you have finished designing the piece, you can be with your family, with friends, or with any group for the repetitive work, the technical part, the stitching and embroidering and stuffing.

So look at your world. Everything around you, every part of nature, every friend or neighbor, every folk or biblical story is a potential source for ideas. It is all there. All you have to do is respond.

2. On Design

RETURN TO ZANZA, wall hanging by the author.

On Design

Most of us have an intuitive sense of design. It is evident in what we refer to as "taste." We say that a certain chair does not fit into a room, or someone's necktie does not go with his suit, or that we like the "lines" of one car better than another. We also recognize when a picture is crooked or when one color does not look well with another. What we are really talking about are relationships, the way elements work with each other.

Design, like penmanship, is partly a personal affair. In our early years at school we are all taught to form the same shapes and symbols in a similar fashion; but gradually our personalities emerge and we find that ways of writing are as varied as people. In design too, each person favors particular colors, values, shapes, lines and textures. Each tends to organize them in ways which become a personal signature.

Your theme will help you to define the design of your piece. If you are true to your theme, the work will have consistency and harmony. One part of the piece will obviously "go with" the other. Sometimes you will do this by creating similarities and sometimes by contrasts. Always think in terms of agreement of parts, of relationships.

SELF PORTRAIT, appliqued quilt by Sharon McKain.

17

CREATING IN CLOTH

Color

Quite often in a design, it is the experience of the colors that strikes us first. Consider the colors of your piece. They might be defined by the theme, by the effect you want to produce, or they might relate to outside needs, such as the decorating scheme of a room. For this you will probably find it helpful to refer to a color wheel. You can use poster paint and paper to construct one. If you prefer, you can find a color wheel in an art book or an art supply store. The color wheel contains the three basic primary colors: red, yellow and blue and mixtures of them. The primary colors stand alone, each separate from one another.

By means of mixtures, a bridge can be established between any two of the primary colors. Between these primary colors, there are endless combinations that can be constructed by continuing the mixing process. Colors that are next to each other on the color wheel will tend to blend; colors opposite each other, complementary colors, tend to clash. You can make good use of blending and clashing, depending on what you want to do.

But just as you would not fill one platter with the same amounts of fruits, vegetables, meats and breads, you would not load your piece with equal varieties of many different

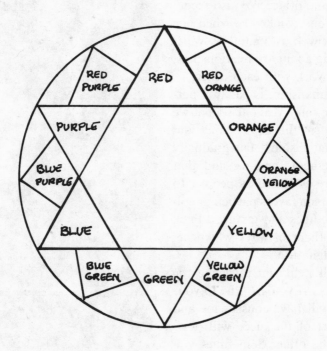

colors. Certain colors should dominate to set the tone, while others should blend or clash with them.

For a pleasing effect you might pick colors that are closely related, i.e., next to each other on the color wheel.

Study a summer landscape. You will see endless varieties of green and just when your eye becomes bored, you will discover small bits of orange or red or yellow. You can do this in your work. Pick a color and see how many variations of it you can combine. For example, you could start with blue and add small amounts of yellow until it becomes green. Then, for interest, add small dashes of red and orange.

Often, colors are classified as "warm" and "cool." Red, yellow, and orange are considered "warm" colors. Blue, green and violet are thought of as "cool" colors. You could develop a color scheme with a basically "warm" or basically "cool" tone.

In terms of depth, warm colors tend to come forward; cool colors tend to recede. Look at a field of flowers. The bright ones seem to pop up at you against the green leaves. Use these principles to create a sense of space.

Intensity is another way of describing color. It means brightness or dullness. Intensity varies depending upon the interaction of colors. The red pillow that seemed so subdued in the store can leap screamingly at you when you get it home and the blue tie that was bright and lively in the store can look devastatingly dull with the wrong suit. These factors all have to do with relationships, with the influence of one color upon the other.

Look at nature and you will see that colors are usually related in their intensity. A fall landscape is brilliant in its myriad of colors;

but all the colors work together because most of them are on the same level of intensity. You can see the same thing happening in the soft tones of winter. The colors are different enough to be interesting and similar enough (through the close range of intensity) to be harmonious.

Value

Value has to do with light and shade. If you take black paint and keep adding white to it you can create a value scale.

The same can be done with a color. Add black or white to a color and you will change its value. For example, by adding increasing amounts of white, red can go through successive shades until it becomes the subtlest pink imaginable.

Value can set the tone of a piece. You can use a large variety of colors and maintain a harmonious effect simply by paying attention to value. For example, if you want a somber mood, you might consider using darker values; for a lighter mood you might consider more of an overall pastel tone. Value creates contrast and interest. Value also creates a sense of depth. Take a cue from nature. Walk outdoors and you will see that when objects move into the distance they seem to fade. If you want to create a sense of depth in your piece, you might utilize this knowledge, using the lighter values for the background.

EASTER BANNER designed by Herbert Borst and made by Joan Heimlich, Barbara Wilkens, and Pat Gerwert. The sunburst is made from red, orange, yellow, and pink felt with purple letters and gold sequins and trimmings.

Since colors have visual "weight," you need to think about balance. Large areas could be comprised of subdued colors; smaller areas might be composed of brighter colors. A warm-toned piece can have small bits of cool colors for variety and contrast.

Emotions play an important part in the use of color. For example, think of how red is used to denote danger. It is also associated with warmth, excitement and blood. In its simplest form, our language expresses this. We say someone is purple with rage or a yellow coward or true blue. There are endless associations of color with emotions. You can use this knowledge as a tool, supporting the emotional content of your subject matter with appropriate colors.

Usually we create our color combinations without thinking about them and most of the time our color sense is effective.

When you create your piece, think in terms of balance, harmony and variety. Experiment with different color relationships. Make one color dominate and work around that, or start with one or two colors and vary the value and intensity, or work with a dark-toned piece and vary the colors. Rely on your intuitive sense and if it does not feel right, trust your feelings. Return to this section to see if you can track down the problem.

And experiment boldly. The worst that can happen is that you have to add another piece of fabric.

Shape

The main feature of an object is its shape. By perceiving shape, we recognize the object. With great economy, an artist can describe a person, a tree, a boat, a landscape, without having to go beyond the barest outlines.

Children, too, perceive and express the shape characteristic of things. In their work, simple shapes carry much meaning.

Your piece of work will depend upon your use of shapes. The shapes themselves, their placement and their relationship to each other, form the structure. In all this, shapes carry color, value, line and texture as well as convey meaning.

Shapes come in an infinite variety. Just by expansion, contraction and decoration, a similar shape can have different meanings.

However, in thinking about variety, remember that for a design to have a feeling of unity it is necessary that its parts relate to one another. I have spoken about this in the section on color, noting that colors can relate by color families (example: blues, blue-reds, blue-yellows, etc.) or by values. The same is true for shapes. Shapes need not repeat themselves endlessly, one looking like a machine-stamped version of the other, but it is important that they bear a resemblance to each other. While still maintaining a degree of sameness, you can vary the size and vary the shape enough so that there is similarity and contrast. Look at a forest. One tree is similar to the other. This principle of relating shapes gives reassurance to anyone looking at your piece. You can look from one part to the other and see a "familiar face." There is enough harmony to feel comfortable that the piece "works" and enough variety to make looking at it interesting.

Also, this kind of repetition gives a won-

PILLOW PEOPLE by the author. These are created from similar basic shapes. The addition of facial

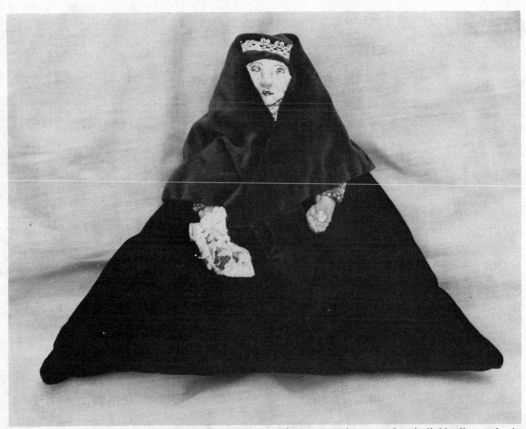

features, hair, and trimmings all serve to give a different character and tone and to individualize each piece.

CREATING IN CLOTH

AFTER THE FALL, wall hanging by the author.

Detail from CELEBRATIONS, a group banner created in a federally-funded workshop, led by the author at the Mark Twain Junior High School for the Gifted and Talented in Brooklyn.

derful internal rhythm. As in the repetition of a musical beat, repeating a form sets up a movement in the piece and one part echoes another.

When you begin working, try to make simple geometric shapes and variations of them. A tree can become a rectangle and a half-circle; people can become triangles and circles.

By using these basic shapes you have only a few elements to be concerned about. You can think primarily of placement and size, or you can dwell on rhythm and proportion. Knowing that shapes have weight, direct your senses to adjusting balance. By using these basic shapes and by repeating them with variations, you can establish a unity (of sameness) and a contrast (of differences). All this establishes order and interest, and artistic wholeness. A good example of this is the way in which the cover of this book was designed. Note the repeat of circular forms, from the objects to the lettering, one gay circle bouncing against the other. Note how the faces relate. Even though they are dissimilar, done in different styles and media by different artists, there is a strong relationship between the faces of the angel, the stuffed doll and the lion tamer.

Remember that shapes can create space, too. Looking at nature again, you see that close objects are larger than those further away. By use of size, placement, and overlapping, we can manipulate the shapes to represent a sense of depth in a fabric hanging.

25

CREATING IN CLOTH

Another thing to remember is that you might fall in love with the shapes themselves, or with a particular shape and ignore what is around it. If you have ever done any photographing, it is easy to see this. You zero in on a person and forget what is around him. When you look at the finished print, you discover strange things in the background or even in front of the figure.

When you place shapes on the background fabric, try to be attentive to the balance of the overall piece. Step back; view it from a distance and from several angles.

Most of the time we sense lack of balance.

I HAVE FOUND THE SHEEP THAT WAS LOST by Sister Helena Steffens-Meier.

We say "something is not quite right" without realizing what that something is. So, trust your judgement. We all have an innate sense of shape-relationship. You can easily judge whether you can fit the car into a certain parking space. You know when a sofa is too massive for the room or when the pattern of the wallpaper does not go with the pattern of the curtains. You can sense if things are top heavy or incorrectly proportioned.

If you run into a snag, this chapter should help you to put your finger on what is wrong. But, in the end, it is your feelings that will decide. Go with them.

CREATING IN CLOTH

Line

In drawing and painting, line defines shape. It is made by pencil, brush, crayon or other tools. In fabric art, line is made in several ways. It can be the edge of the shape, created by the path of your scissors as you cut out a form, or it can be the path that thread and yarn take when you embroider and embellish your work. Line creates boundaries, separating one shape from the other; or it creates bridges as it moves across the piece. Line creates rhythm and balance.

When lines are placed close together, they enrich a surface. They create different textures and patterns. They create lights and darks. They create depth.

Lines, like shapes and colors, can reflect emotions. Soaring vertical lines are thought to be stately. Horizontal lines are considered restful. Oblique lines seem dynamic.

When people work with applique, they often forget that they are using line as well as color, value, shape, and texture. While you may not wish to stress line as much as some of the other elements, it is still helpful to know that line influences what is around it.

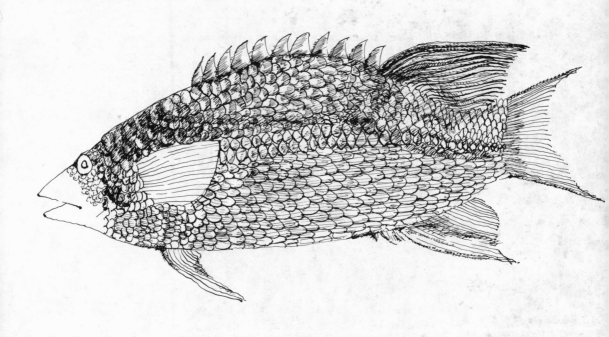

Detail from BEHOLD THE HANDMAID by Sister Helena Steffens-Meier.

Texture

Texture is the play of surfaces. The texture of a fabric depends upon how it was created and what fibers were used. Texture is intrinsic to fiber art. It establishes richness and variety. It can be beautiful to look at as well as exciting to touch. Enjoy the textural interplay between surfaces, not only with fabric alone, but with different threads and yarns as well as with stuffing and quilting.

Try to contrast the rough and smooth, shiny and dull, the close and loosely woven.

There is a wealth of fabrics and threads from which to choose.

Your total design will depend upon how you organize and combine its different parts, its colors, values, shapes, lines, and textures. This organization will develop naturally as you work.

The forthcoming chapters will discuss translating ideas into banners, quilts, and soft objects. But, before going on to these projects, it might be helpful for you to know about materials you will want to use.

CREATING IN CLOTH

3. Tools and Materials

ST. MATTHEW from the HOLY SPIRIT RETABLE by Virginia Churchill Bath.

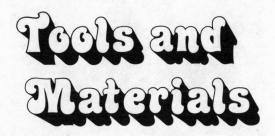

Tools and Materials

For fabric art you do not have to invest in many supplies nor build an extra room to work in. Most of the materials you need are right in your home. They are not messy and do not take up much space. You can work anywhere and anytime the mood strikes you. Everything is portable and, since techniques are generally uncomplicated, you do not have to keep working on only one piece for an extended period of time.

The materials and tools you need are those things which you normally keep around for sewing projects. A basic list includes fabrics, pins, needles, thread, thimble, scissors, tape measure, iron, embroidery thread, yarn, trimmings and fabric glue. An embroidery hoop and a sewing machine are optional. For specific projects, such as quilting, supplies might include a ruler, cardboard, carbon paper, tracing paper, graph paper, large sheets of drawing or newsprint paper for patterns, filler (stuffing or quilt batting), and a quilting frame or hoop.

Because there is such a tremendous variety of fabrics, you might try browsing around a fabric store to help familiarize yourself with different materials and tools. Look through everything from fabrics to yarns, from ribbons to threads. Look at the sequins and the trimmings. Look at the needles and scissors. A fabric store is a fantastic treasure chest. Just think about the diversity of texture, the vibrations and harmonies between different colors, and the wide range of imaginative patterns.

Fabric

Before buying anything, you should take stock of what you already own. Keep a scrap bag of bits and pieces left over from sewing projects, old articles of clothing you hate to part with, curtains that never seemed to fit right, and any other odd fabrics. These unmatched pieces are particularly wonderful for small projects such as quilt blocks and pillows.

If you do not already have a scrap bag, check with your neighbors and friends or, if you teach, ask the students to bring in fabric scraps. People hate to throw away good pieces of fabric and trimmings. You might be the grateful recipient of beautiful bits of donated cloth that someone else can not use.

Some people keep certain fabrics for nostalgic reasons, particularly old clothing: a child's first party dress, a husband's or son's tie, a grandmother's apron. If you have saved

CREATING IN CLOTH

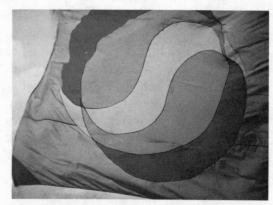

TWO FLAGS by Anders Holmquist.

some of these and use them in your work, they will always bring pleasant memories and not be hidden in storage.

It is up to you to decide how to use what you own, but be certain that the fabric is not so thin and worn that it will disintegrate. Many have old quilts and find to their sorrow that some fragile piece is worn beyond repair. You are not going to save money by using poor material. Do not consider even your first try as mere practice, because if you invest your time, energy and love in your project, it is worthwhile to have decent materials with which to work.

I prefer new materials. They are easy to manipulate. For most of my work, the most suitable fabrics are those with "body" such as medium weight muslins, cottons, linens, and various blends. I shy away from wools because moths have damaged two of my woolen banners. To this basic list I often add silks and satins, velvets, rayons, chintz and brocades. Occasionally, if the piece warrants, I use felt.

Actually felt is a good material for anyone to use, but especially for very young children. The colors are bright and bold. Felt has no fraying edges to turn under and sewing on it is easy. For those who do not sew, felt can be glued with a fabric glue, and all sorts of trimmings can be added.

You will enjoy experimenting with different types of fibers and weaves, but generally try to avoid materials such as monk's cloth,

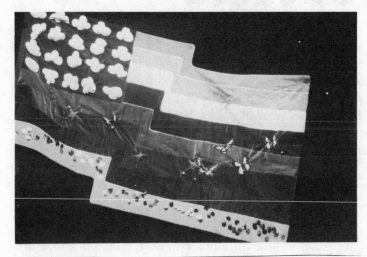

RAINBOW FLAG by Sas Colby.

burlap, and other open weaves, because they sag or fray easily. It is possible to embellish with bits of these fabrics, but structurally they are not very strong and cannot carry or back the whole work.

For hand sewing, natural fibers are the most manageable. I find the fabric blends to be too resistant to my needle, and generally I dislike the way they feel when I sew. You may not agree. Experiment with different kinds of fabric before you decide.

If you are going to create a banner or flag for outdoor use, it must be sturdy and able to withstand the wind and rain. Suitable fabrics are canvas, nylon, and oilcloth.

Since most banners are generally not washed, you can seek a wide range of materials which might even include non-fabrics, such as pieces of wood, metal, beads, nuts, bells, feathers, shells, bones, raffia, dried pods, driftwood, and other found objects.

Detail from OF TIME AND SPACE, wall hanging by the author.

CREATING IN CLOTH

Pins and Needles

Generally, it is easier to pin pieces to their backing and not bother to baste, except on special occasions where absolute precision is necessary. Whether I am sewing by hand or machine, I like to use long dressmaker pins when they are available. Other pins are suitable, too.

The choice of needles should be left to your own good sense and comfort. Choose needles that thread easily and pass through cloth with little effort. Maintain a supply of "sharps" and crewel or embroidery needles. The sharps are good for general hand sewing and for applique, because their thin eyes can be threaded with mercerized cotton thread.

Embroidery needles with their larger eyes are suitable for sewing with embroidery thread. Occasionally I use chenille (sharp-tipped, large-eyed) needles for thick threads and tapestry wool. For quilting, the short, thin quilting needles called "betweens" are excellent.

For very young children it is best to use blunt-tipped plastic or metal tapestry needles with large eyes. Such needles are used mainly with open-weave fabrics because they pierce closely woven fabrics with difficulty.

Thimbles

The use of a thimble is up to you. I cannot sew without one and would recommend that you use one. But, here again, do what you consider comfortable.

Tape Measures and Rulers

A carpenter's metal tape measure which springs back into itself is a fine hand tool. It is invaluable for measuring everything from quilt blocks to figuring out the width of the fabric frame. However, any tape measure will do. The soft plastic or cloth ones are fine. A metal ruler is most accurate and best for making quilt block patterns and for making any straight edges.

Irons

There are all sorts of good irons on the market. You need something that will press out a wrinkle or press open a seam. Any iron that you own which works for you is satisfactory.

Trimmings

Your selection of trimmings is infinite, and they do not have to be bought. Collect

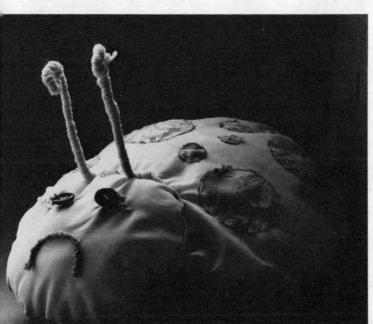

LADYBUG, soft object created in a workshop led by the author at the Katonah Elementary School under the auspices of the Katonah Gallery and the New York State Council for the Arts.

odds and ends of everything: buttons, bells, twine, ribbons, tassels, laces, beads, tiny mirrors, bits of metal and anything else you can sew or glue onto fabric.

Only the use of the piece limits the variety of trimmings. If you are making a washable item, you will want to carefully chose your trimmings. If you are making a banner, a stuffed Christmas tree ornament or any non-washable item, you can choose from a much wider range of materials.

Fabric Glue

White Sobo glue, which is available in most fabric and hobby stores, is excellent. If you cannot find Sobo, there are many other good white glues, including Elmer's, which are suitable.

Embroidery Hoops

These double hoops serve to keep the fabric smooth for embroidering. They come in different diameters, so that you can fit one to the size of the piece you are working on. Although embroidery hoops are available in wood, metal or plastic, you may want the long-lived wooden hoops which have a screw at one end to tighten the hoop. Since children love every new kind of apparatus, they as well as adults enjoy using hoops. To prevent creasing the material, do not forget to pull your work out of the hoop once you have stopped sewing.

Sewing Machines

The choice of whether of not to use a sewing machine is up to you. Sewing machines are great timesavers, particularly for piecing and finishing a quilt.

Machine stitching is excellent for sturdy construction. It is strong and regular and particulary appropriate in the creation of pillows and soft toys. But in most cases, it is what feels right, largely a matter of taste, which determines whether you sew by machine or by hand.

I prefer the look and feel of hand-sewn objects. It is great fun to look at the stitches and to envision the personality of the stitcher. Besides, there is nothing more enjoyable than sitting with friends and family in a relaxed and comfortable atmosphere, with fabric in hand, stitching slowly, bit by bit. And of course, there is the lively and pleasurable experience of hand sewing a quilt in a sociable group.

When you see suggestions for various ways to finish, you can decide whether or not you need a sewing machine.

If you already own a sewing machine, its basic straight stitch is adequate for most projects. However, if you are going to buy a new machine, look for one with a good zigzag stitch which tightens down to a close satin stitch. Most new machines have this feature. If you want to do fancier work, there are a number of machines that do many other kinds of decorative embroidery stitches as well.

Remember, though, a machine is not an absolute necessity. Much beautiful work was done years before sewing machines were ever invented.

Threads

Cotton mercerized or cotton wrapped polyester sewing threads are best for most projects. I keep an assortment of these in different colors for both hand and machine sewing. For quilting there are special quilting

CREATING IN CLOTH

Teachers, staff, and friends at the Matthew Peterson School creating a baby quilt as a surprise gift for Jo Anne Tritto. Each designed and executed a square and helped put the whole together.

threads which, because of their waxed coating, are stiff and smooth and do not tangle. They also come in a variety of colors. You can use the mercerized cotton or polyester threads for quilting, but if you do so, coat them with beeswax which is available in any sewing store.

For embroidery, I especially like the shiny, bright quality of the cotton pearl or silk. But, when you embellish your piece with decorative stitching, first determine its function and whether or not it must be washable. Otherwise, your choice is unlimited. You might try silken threads or crewel wools; experiment, too, with metallic threads and bits of handspun yarns.

Scissors

A good pair of well-sharpened 6″ to 8″ scissors is all you really need. Be certain that you are comfortable with them. If they easily fit into your hand, and cut the fabric without catching any threads, you need no other fabric scissors. Some find the new plastic-handled scissors more comfortable, but I still prefer to use my old steel scissors for most of my work. Never use fabric scissors to cut paper, for paper dulls scissors, and it is vital to keep your scissors sharp.

As you go along, you may want other types of scissors for special needs, such as small, pointed embroidery scissors for embroidery, or thread clips for machine sewing. However, one good pair for cutting fabric will serve you very well.

Fillers

There are all sorts of materials on the market for stuffing soft toys, dolls, pillows, and quilts. The most common types are of dacron or polyester fiber, shredded foam and kapok. These fillers come pre-packaged and are easily obtainable in fabric, craft and variety stores. Generally, dacron is the best filler. It is washable, non-allergenic, and stuffs easily. Others shift and lump when washed. Shredded foam is popular with school groups because it is less expensive, but it is messy to work with.

New quilting filler is available in the form of sheets of dacron batting which is easy to use. You can use an old blanket, or a piece of flannel instead of the polyester batting, but it will not be as puffy, and here again it may shift and become lumpy when washed.

Quilting Hoops and Frames

Quilting hoops look like embroidery hoops, but are larger. They are round, made of wood and have a metal screw at one end. They serve to keep the quilt sandwich of top, filler and backing smooth, so that they can be sewn together. These double hoops are most useful for quilting small pieces, but can be used for a larger project if the parts are first basted carefully.

Quilting frames can accommodate full-size quilts. Most quilting frames can be taken apart and put back together easily for storage and mobility. Quilting hoops and frames are available in the fabric section of large department stores or can be obtained through fabric or hobby shops.

Hoops or frames are not absolute necessities. There are quilters who work comfortably, with their quilt right on their laps. However, it is important to carefully baste the

39

three layers together so that they do not slip around as you work.

If you do not own a particular material or tool, try another. Improvise. If you cannot do something one way, do it in another way. Think of the next few chapters as a guide. Try my suggestions. If they work for you, fine. If not, try your own way.

*to make
off hand or* [handwritten]

4. Banners and Wall Hangings

CREATING IN CLOTH

REALTIME, wall hanging by the author. Courtesy of Milena and Fred Jelinek.

Banners and Wall Hangings

What kind of banner will you create? Will it be functional or purely decorative? Will it be a church banner or a civic banner? Will it be used to celebrate a family event or for playing a game? Will it be carried in a procession, hung on a wall or flown like a flag? Will it be created by an adult or a child, by a group or an individual?

Assembling Materials

To construct a banner you will need a background fabric and materials to applique over it. Calculating the yardage of your background fabric is easy. First, estimate the size of the finished banner. If it is going to hang in a specific spot, measure the space beforehand. If it will be held in a procession, make certain it is of a size suitable for carrying.

To the estimated dimensions of the banner, add an extra 1/2″ all around to attach a border.

The background fabric must have enough body and weight to support the applique pieces. If you are using a lightweight cotton for your background piece, line it with another cloth or double your fabric before you sew. Since this will be of the same size as your background fabric, add it to your total calculations.

Next, think about colors. What is the dominant mood of your banner? How and where will it be used? Let your theme guide your selection of colors.

You may want to experiment with using prints. A good rule of thumb is to use small, overall prints. Generally, these do not dominate the work when seen from afar and when seen close up, they lend interest.

After you have assembled your fabrics, it is a good idea to iron them smooth. Now, with your materials in hand, you are ready to work. Cut your background fabric to the finished size and shape plus the seam allowance. The selvage should run vertically so that the banner does not sag.

Planning and Cutting

Do you prefer working from a pattern? You can start with a small sketch, photograph, or illustration. Or, create a collage of colored papers by cutting shapes and moving them around on a background shape until you have a pleasing arrangement. If you would like to refresh your memory about design arrangement, check back with chapter two.

Then, create a large reproduction of your small sketch. The reproduction should be the

PALM SUNDAY
PROCESSIONAL
BANNER, one of a series of banners created
as part of a group project under the direction
of Wilna Lane for the
Mt. Kisco Presbyterian
Church.

size you want your finished banner to be. Draw your reproduction onto brown paper or newspaper. Think in terms of approximating your sketch, not of copying it line for line. When your reproduction has been drawn, cut out the shapes and use them as patterns. Pin each pattern to the cloth, and cut it out. If the applique piece is to be sewn by hand, allow an extra 3/8″ all around for the hem. If it is going to be attached by machine, you can cut it to size without the extra seam allowance. After it has been cut, pin

44

STUDENTS AT A BANNER MAKING WORKSHOP, led by the author at Fox
Lane High School under the auspices of the Katonah Gallery and the N.Y. State
Council of the Arts

each applique piece to the fabric background.

If you like to work freely, make believe
your scissors are a drawing tool and cut as
you go along. Then, the procedure is the
same as described above: position each fabric
piece on the background fabric and pin it in
place.

If you like to work in an upright position,
tack your background fabric to a wall. In
that way it is easy to stand back and look at
the work from a distance. It is especially
helpful to work this way when you are creating a large banner.

Of course, it is just as easy to work when
looking down. Find a large enough work
space, a table or perhaps the floor. The way
you work is dependent upon your preference,
and the space you have.

It is great fun to watch your ideas develop
as your banner grows piece by piece. Unlike
patchwork (which has a few surprises also),
nothing is ever fully determined in advance.
You start with a general idea, but as you cut
and pin, wonderful things begin to happen.
Fabric and color create new and exciting
combinations. Sizes and spaces change;
shapes become altered. The piece starts to
come to life and gradually it takes on a life
of its own.

And this is all so tentative. So far, the
pieces of fabric are only pinned down. Is that
shape too awkward or too dominant? You
can unpin it, take it away, and cut another
piece to substitute. Is that color too bright?
Take it off and add another or try adding
another applique piece right over it so that
only the edges of the original piece show.

45

CREATING IN CLOTH

Detail from QUILTED WALL HANGING, by the author. Note the mixture of techniques including applique, quilting and stitchery by hand and machine and the hand drawing of figures with the use of permanent markers.

This casual quality of creating in cloth is one of its greatest advantages. Move your pieces around until you feel the banner looks right. There is nobody here to tell you that you have made a mistake.

As you progress with pinning and cutting, other techniques may come into your mind.

You can paint cloth by using acrylics or any of the fabric paints or dyes available from art supply stores. You can also use permanent felt markers to draw part of the design.

You might want to experiment with reverse applique. This is a method of creating design in fabric by cutting away, rather than adding on. Three or four layers of different colored cottons are basted together and then designs are cut through each layer to expose the color underneath. The raw edges are turned under and hemmed. Occasionally, small bits of fabric are added in certain areas to heighten the design.

Do you want a chance to think about the banner before it becomes permanently stitched? It is perfectly appropriate to put your work aside and to come back to it days or weeks later. Just be sure the applique pieces have been carefully pinned, then fold the banner and put it away for a while.

Group Projects

For group projects the technical aspects are similar to individual projects; however, there are some other things to be considered. Begin by agreeing on a theme. Religious themes, holiday themes, themes from nature or historical themes are all appropriate to group projects.

Whenever possible, have a meeting to plan the banner. If members of the group freely

RED AND BLUE by the author. Applique and reverse applique wall hanging stretched on a wooden frame.

vent their ideas, much originality and freshness will emerge. As a teacher, I am always amazed at the new and simple suggestions that come out of a group. One idea leads to another and suddenly I am hearing something I never thought of before.

A group needs to agree on standards beforehand, but there should be flexibility and allowance for individual preferences. Particularly with children's work, it is necessary to permit a wide range of individual differences. You can show them the way, but you must allow them to experience things and express them in their own manner. Each person has his or her own tastes, vi-

sions, and capabilities. A group project should always respect the individual and allow for personal expression and contribution.

A group can construct a banner as if it were a mural. Tack or staple the background fabric to a wall and have people cut and pin their applique pieces to it. Or, think about having each person create his or her own small banner. Agree upon a uniform size for each and decide on the choice of fabric and colors if you think it necessary. Later, the large banner can be constructed by assembling these individual blocks in much the same way you would put together a quilt.

CIRCUS BANNER, a group banner created in a federally funded workshop led by the author at the Mark Twain Junior High School for the Gifted and Talented in Brooklyn.

When everything has been assembled and pinned or basted, and the banner looks the way you want it to look, you are ready to sew. With very young children you may suggest gluing, but for others, sewing is the most attractive and most durable way to secure the applique pieces.

You can applique by hand or by machine. You will find there is a great difference between that smooth, finished edge with the interesting stitchery and the raw unfinished piece you started with.

Stitching

If you are going to applique by hand, turn the applique pieces under and hold them with your thumb as you sew. Do not double your thread. Always use a single strand. Use a running stitch or a blindstitch.

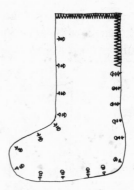

For pointed corners, first turn down one edge, then the top, and finally the other edge. Use a straight stitch to hold the point.

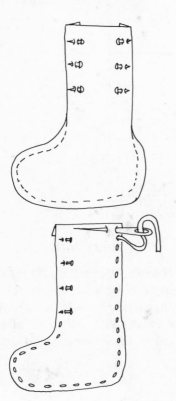

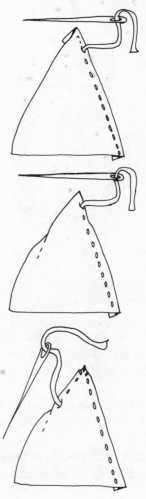

49

If you want to curve an edge inward, clip close to the seam allowance and then turn the edge under.

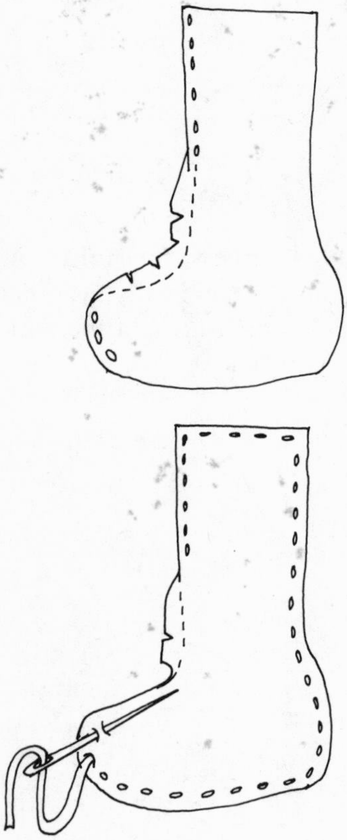

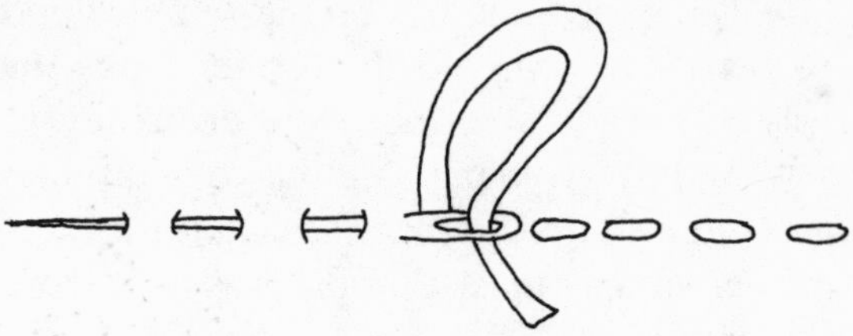

RUNNING STITCH

BACK STITCH

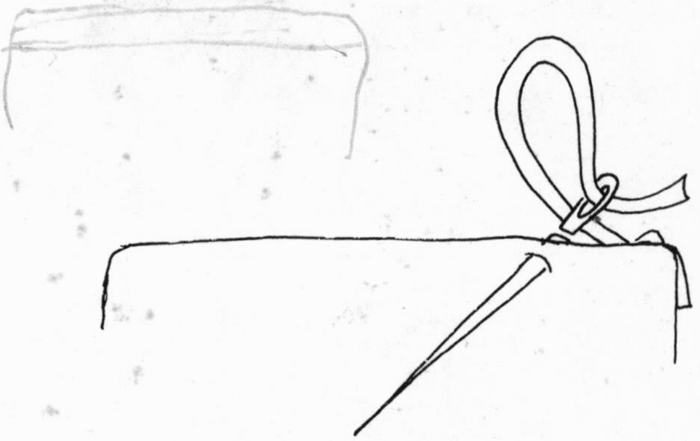

How to applique a curved edge.

BLIND STITCH

The most useful stitches for applique are the following:

Running stitches are a series of small neat stitches evenly spaced. They are used both for attaching applique pieces and for quilting.

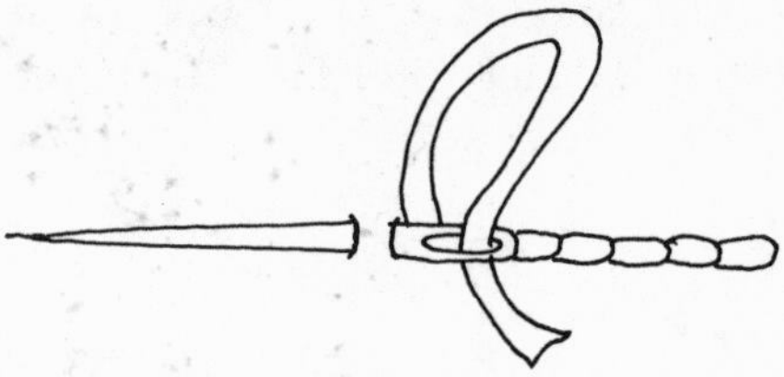

The back stitch is a variation of the running stitch. It is a sturdy stitch, used to make seams.

The blind stitch is a hidden hemming stitch. It can be used for attaching applique pieces.

Hand Embroidery Stitches

Embroidery stitches enrich the fabric surface. They can be used singly for one effect and grouped side by side or overlapped for another effect. Whether used alone or in combination, the six most useful stitches are:

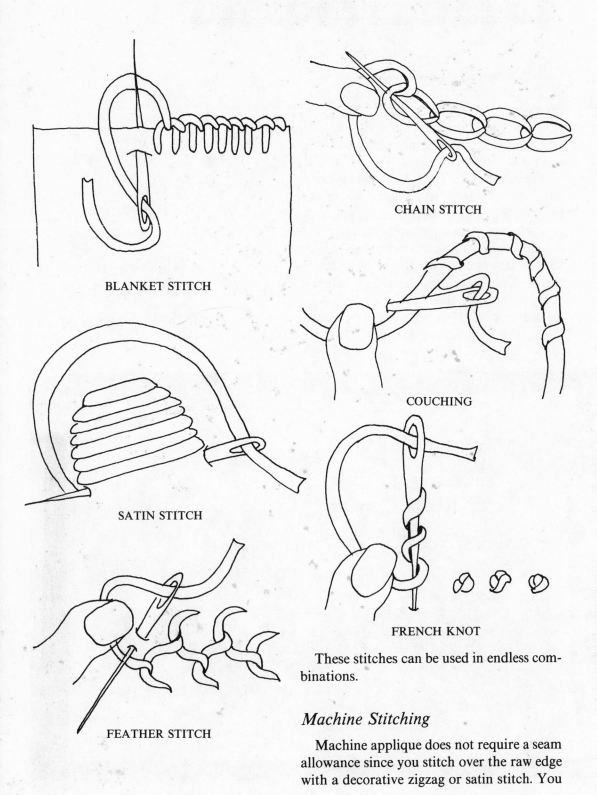

BLANKET STITCH

CHAIN STITCH

COUCHING

SATIN STITCH

FRENCH KNOT

FEATHER STITCH

These stitches can be used in endless combinations.

Machine Stitching

Machine applique does not require a seam allowance since you stitch over the raw edge with a decorative zigzag or satin stitch. You

51

CREATING IN CLOTH

may find it just as easy to pin each piece instead of basting it. Place the pins at right angles to the fabric and sew directly over them.

If you find your fabric puckering as you sew, remove it from the machine and pin a piece of brown wrapping paper to the back of your work. This will give the background fabric extra weight. Afterwards, when you have finished sewing the piece, the paper can be easily ripped away from the back.

For decorative machine stitching, it may be necessary to cover the feed plate or lower the pressure or change the adjustment for darning, so that the fabric can be easily pushed back and forth. Check your machine manual for specific directions.

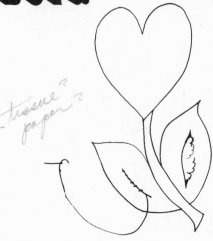

TRAPUNTO

Using Stuffing in Banners

While you are appliqueing your pieces to the background, think about whether or not

Wall hanging adapted from GODEY'S LADIES BOOK by Gladys Boalt.

52

you are going to embellish your piece and how you will do it. If you are going to use stuffing to enrich the surface, you can resort to a trapunto technique after the piece has been completed, or you can stuff the applique pieces as you go along.

Trapunto is actually a quilting method by which small areas of a piece of work are padded to create texture, depth and an overall decorative feeling. It is not limited to quilts, but is a technique suitable to banners and soft pieces. Decide which applique pieces you want to stuff, then turn over the banner, make a small slit, stuff it with filler and then sew the opening together.

For another kind of padded effect you could quilt your banner.

Later, after the applique pieces are permanently sewn, you can use decorative stitches and add trimmings. Add bits of glitter and sequins, beads, shells, yarns, bells and any other trimmings you may have collected. If they cannot be sewn, glue them down with white glue. Make sure everything is well fastened before you go on to finishing the edges and mounting the banner.

VIEW FROM FRANCES' WINDOW, quilted and stuffed wall hanging by the author.

53

Finishing

There are various ways to finish your banner. You can border it with other fabric, sew ready-made blanket binding around it, or simply turn the edges under and hem them. The object is to give your banner a finished look and to make it possible to hang. Choose a technique that appeals to you and that is suitable to your banner.

A technique for finishing a banner is to border the piece, turn the border under, hem it to itself and then attach another fabric to the back as a lining.

Or, cut a backing for your banner the same size as the banner itself. With right sides together, sew these pieces to each other, leaving an opening at the bottom. Then turn the whole thing inside out, hem the bottom and press.

If it suits the style of your banner and if you have bells or tassels to add, you can tack them onto the bottom edges.

A simple way to prepare a banner for hanging or to adapt a quilt for wall display is to sew loops into the top. Place the ends of the loops between the lining and the front. And, if you use felt, it is easy to

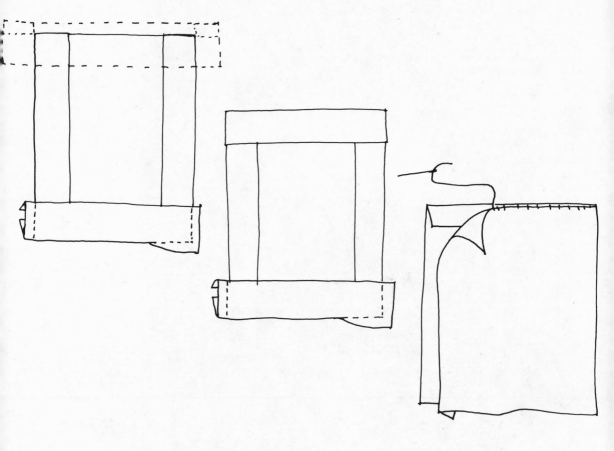

cut loops in a variety of shapes out of the top edge. If you want to create a casing for a dowel, turn the top edge over and sew across the top.

Hanging the Banner

The way in which you will mount your banner depends upon its function. A wall hanging should be suspended from a wooden or metal dowel or a flat wooden strip which is pushed through loops or casings or stapled on. These wooden dowels should be sanded and stained or painted. Their ends can be finished with finials or knobs.

To suspend your banner from the wall, add screw eyes to each end or drill a hole in each end. Then, tie fishline through the holes, and hang the banner from a hook on the wall.

Often, the bottom of the banner does not hang smoothly. This is natural when working with cloth, but if the soft rippled bottom is not to your liking, you can construct a casing or add some loops onto the bottom for a dowel or wooden strip to pass through. This weighted bottom will create a smoother looking finish.

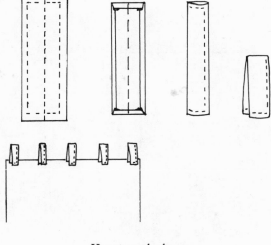

How to make loops
and create a casing.

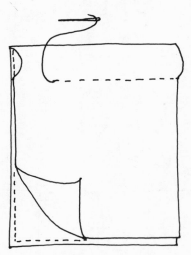

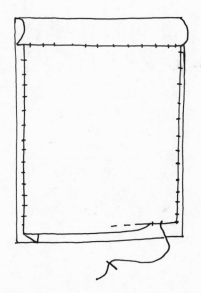

How to make a border and attach a backing.

55

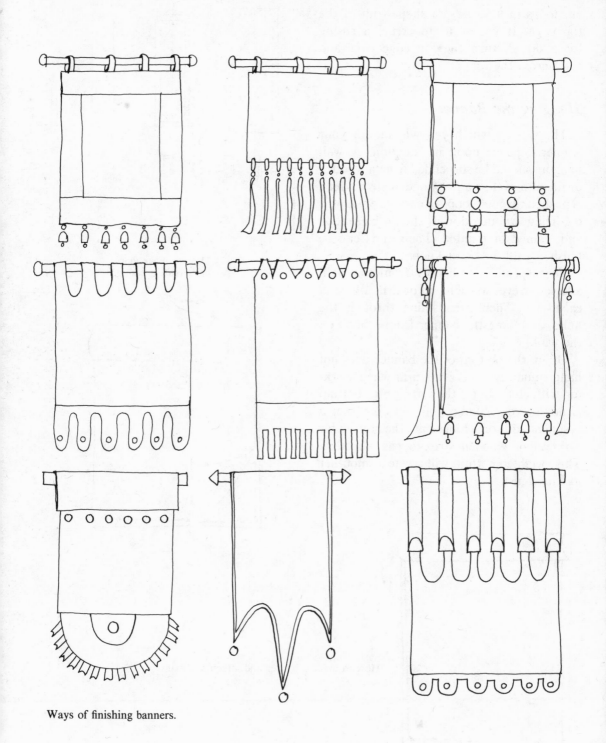

Ways of finishing banners.

GOOD FRIDAY BANNER designed by Philip Franz and executed by a group of women from the First Presbyterian Church of Yorktown.

I AM THE BREAD OF LIFE, designed and executed by Philip Franz.

If your banner is to hang outdoors, treat it the same way as you would an indoor wall hanging. Create a casing for a dowel or thread the banner onto a horizontally hung flagpole. Or, turn the top edge over a wooden strip and staple it. You can also suspend the banner between two trees or nail it to the side of a building.

Mounting a banner for processionals is as simple as mounting it on a wall. Staple the banner to a dowel and hold it like a flag or construct a cross out of two flat strips of wood. Attach the top of the banner to a wooden crossbar by adding loops to the back of the banner or by stapling it on.

You may, if you wish, frame your banner in a rigid wooden frame. Some people prefer to frame a banner because they want it to look like a painting or "fabric picture."

The way to frame your banner with wood is to first stretch the banner onto a rectangle constructed out of artist's canvas stretchers available in assorted sizes in any art supply store. These stretchers are pieces of wood which come in a variety of sizes and are made to interlock. The banner is then stapled onto the stretchers. The most systematic way to do this is to tack opposite sides. Start by tacking the middle of one side and then pull the opposite side and tack that. Then do the same with the top and bottom. Continue to tack all sides outward to the corners in the same way.

After the banner is mounted onto the stretchers, flat wooden strips called lattice stripping (not to be confused with the cloth lattice strips used on quilts) are nailed to all sides to create a frame. Wood lattice stripping can be purchased in any lumberyard, then sanded and stained for an attractive finish. You can also purchase ribbon or twill tape to stretch or tack around the edges for a frame.

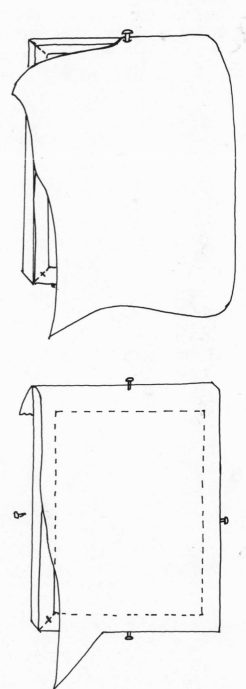

Attaching a banner to a stretcher.

CREATING IN CLOTH

How ever you choose to create and finish your banner, remember that you can adapt many different techniques. The above instructions are not exhaustive. There are other techniques and possibilities. Look through the next few chapters to see if there are new and different possibilities you can utilize.

5. Quilting

PUTNAM COUNTY BICENTENNIAL QUILT, designed and created under the direction of Gladys Boalt.
Gladys Boalt © 1976.

Creating a full-size quilt is not a difficult task, but it does require certain sewing skills and careful, precise measuring. It is also a rather time-consuming project.

Small Projects

If you are a cautious person who plans and tests extensively before you begin a project, it makes sense to start by quilting a small piece. For example, in one evening you could create a charming little pot holder by hand. You would practice the technique of patchwork or applique, or a combination of both, and from there you could go on to larger items. Basically, the ways of working, whether they be with large or small items, are pretty much the same.

Small items like pot holders are also ideal projects for school groups. Youngsters tend to get bored quilting larger units. Creating a smaller item will give them quiltmaking experience without having to work for an overly long time. And pot holders make lovely gifts.

Quilted Pot Holder

Plan to create a nine inch square pot holder. You will need an assortment of colored pieces of cotton for the top, a 10 1/2″ square piece of muslin for the backing and a 9″ square piece of filler which can be batting, part of an old towel, or a piece of blanket. Make certain the fabrics are washed and ironed before beginning.

If this is to be an appliqued top, cut a piece of fabric 9″ square and place your applique pieces on it. When you are satisfied with your design, pin the pieces and then sew them permanently to the top piece of fabric. Go on to "Assembling the 'Sandwich' " and "Tufting" or "Quilting Patterns" sections of this chapter.

Crazy Quilt Pot Holder

A crazy quilt is a cover made up of irregularly-shaped pieces of small, unmatched bits of fabric joined in a random fashion. If your potholder is to be a crazy quilt top, cut one piece of fabric 9″ square and pin the small bits of irregularly shaped pieces of cotton fabric onto it. Start from one corner and baste each piece after tucking under the raw edges. Then sew them with a zigzag or other embroidery stitch such as a blanket stitch, a feather stitch, or some other decorative stitch described in the banner and applique chapter.

Assemble the "sandwich" (p. 68) and finish by tufting or quilting as described later in this chapter.

CREATING IN CLOTH

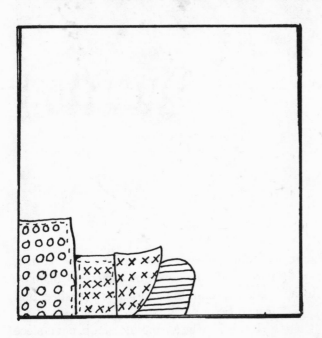

Steps in assembling the top of a crazy quilt block.

Patchwork Pot Holder

You may decide to create a patchwork pot holder. Patchwork is a pieced quilt composed of geometric shapes sewn together with a running stitch by machine or with a backstitch by hand. After the pieces are joined, they are treated as a unit.

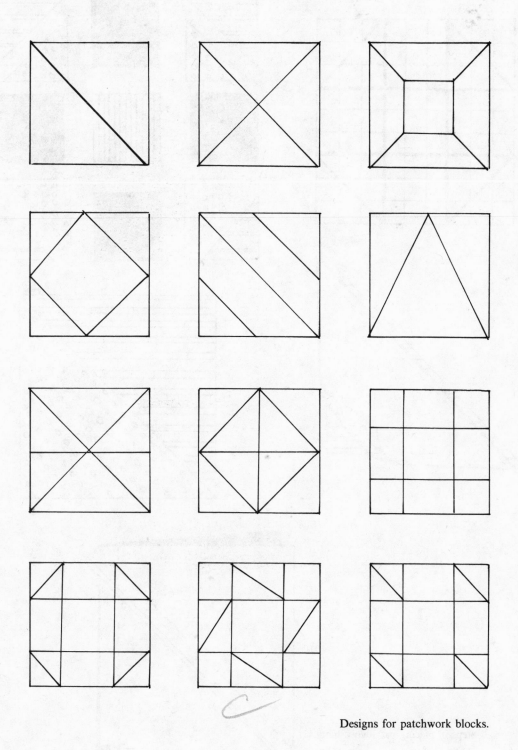

Designs for patchwork blocks.

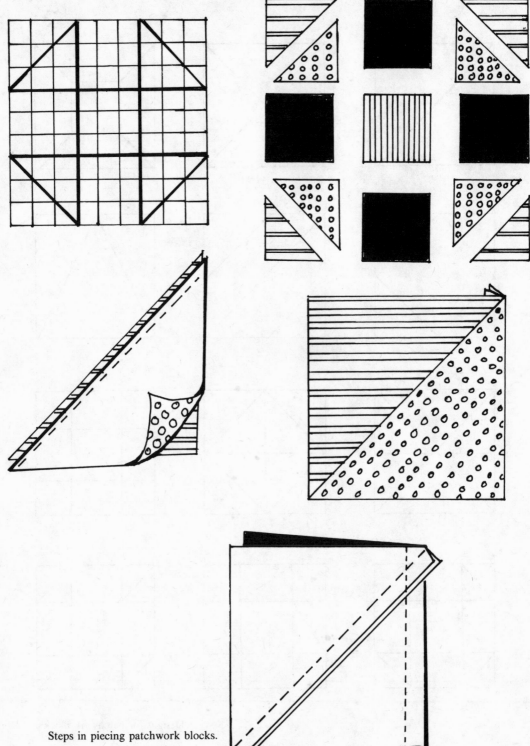

Steps in piecing patchwork blocks.

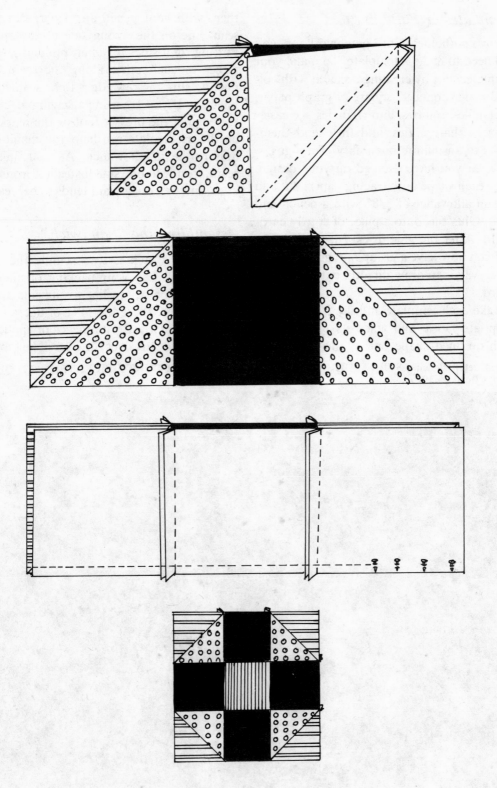

CREATING IN CLOTH

Templates or Patterns

For a potholder with a patchwork top, you will need to make a template. To make your template, start by creating a sketch with colored pencils on a 9″ square of graph paper. Rectangles, squares, and triangles are easier to piece than circles, and they lend themselves to an infinite possibility of designs.

When you have decided on your design, trace each shape onto tracing paper, but add a seam allowance of 3/8″ with a pencil and ruler. Glue this onto a piece of sturdy cardboard. After the glue dries, cut each shape, and you now have a group of templates. Another way is to draw directly onto the cardboard.

Take each template and lay it on the appropriate fabric and trace its outline. Cut each outlined shape out of the fabric and then, with your pencil and ruler, mark the seam line on the wrong side of each piece. Putting right sides together, pin and sew the pieces to each other along the seam line, making sure the raw edges to be seamed are lined up. If you are using a sewing machine, the edge of the presser foot or the markings on the needleplate can help you maintain a uniform seam allowance. As you finish a seam, iron it to one side instead of ironing it open, since an open seam tends to be weaker.

Assembling the "Sandwich"

Your next step is to assemble the quilt "sandwich." Lay your backing of plain or printed cotton or muslin, wrong side up, on a flat surface. Place the filler of dacron batting on top of it and your pieced or appliqued top, right side up, over the filler. The top and

Basted detail showing SYBIL LUDINGTON from the PUTNAM COUNTY BICENTENNIAL QUILT Gladys Boalt © 1976.

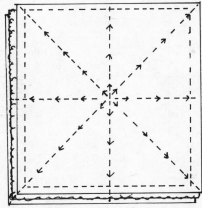

Assembling the sandwich and basting.

Tufting or Tying

Tufting is the easiest and fastest way to attach the three layers. Use thick thread or yarn to tie the layers together at regular intervals. The tufting knots can be placed along the grid made by the basting stitches, which should be removed after the tufting is finished.

Quilting Patterns

If you choose to quilt your piece rather than tuft it, this is a good time to think about the quilting pattern. If you have created an appliqued or patchwork top, you should draw a quilting pattern appropriate to your design. You may find it easier to do this be-

filler should be centered so that there is a 3/4″ excess of backing all around. Top and filler should be the same size. Pin and then baste all three layers together. It is customary to baste through all layers from the center out to the corners, from the center out to the sides, then around all the sides.

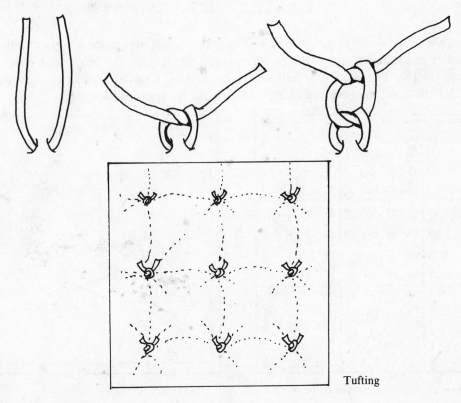

Tufting

CREATING IN CLOTH

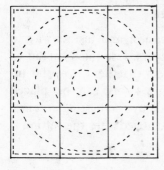
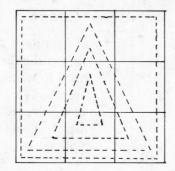
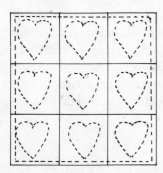
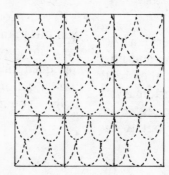

Quilting designs

fore the quilt "sandwich" is assembled. Using pencil or chalk, lightly draw the pattern directly on the top. The pencil line will wash off and the chalk can be brushed away.

You could also place a cup or some other rigid shape over the block and trace a pattern. Any kind of simple geometric shape would be appropriate.

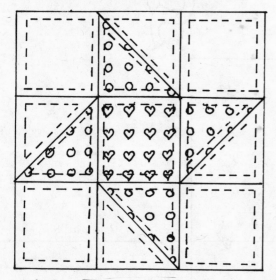

Quilting patterns which follow the shape of the patchwork and applique designs.

For an applique design, or even a pieced top, quilting can follow the shape of the pieces themselves. You might not even have to draw a design, just sew around the outside or the inside of each applique piece.

Now you are ready to quilt by using a small running stitch following your quilting pattern.

Quilting

Space the running stitches evenly to follow the quilting pattern. Take a few stitches at a time before pulling your thread through or, if you want to work more carefully, take a half-stitch at a time by pulling the needle and thread from top to bottom and then from bottom to top.

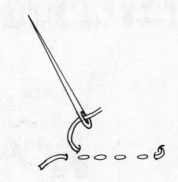

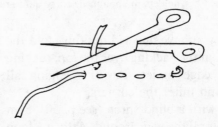

back through the middle layer to lock it in. Then, cut off the tail with scissors. Do not break it.

To end off, make two stitches in the same

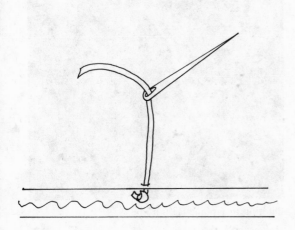

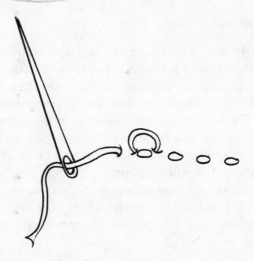

When you are quilting, pull the knot through the bottom layer into the filler, so that your knot does not show.

Or, leaving a long tail of thread, take some running stitches and take one long stitch

place by taking one stitch and then stitching again in the same holes.

Keep checking the back layer to make sure there is no bunching. You can quilt in your lap, with a hoop, or on a frame.

CREATING IN CLOTH

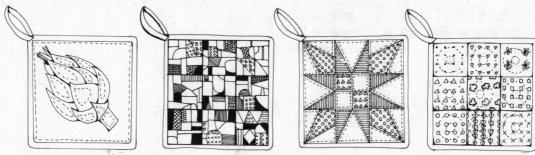

Finished pot holders in appliqued, crazy quilt and patchwork designs.

When you have finished quilting, fold the excess from the backing over the top, tucking the raw edge under. Pin this edging all around and miter the corners.

Then, with a blind stitch (see p. 50), hem the border all the way around. Attach a loop of cording or ribbon and you have finished your first quilted item. Another way of finishing is to attach purchased bias binding and hem it all around.

Pillows

If you would like to make something larger than a pot holder, but smaller than a quilt, consider creating a pillow. Decide on the size of the pillow and add two inches all around. This amount is needed for the seam allowance and because the pillow becomes smaller when it is stuffed. Wash and iron all fabrics you will be using.

Construct your pillow top in the same way you would the pot holder, from assembling the top layer through quilting or tufting, but do not finish the edge.

For the back of the pillow, cut a piece of fabric the same size as the top. The laundering requirements of the back fabric should be

Quilting in lap and with a hoop.

PILLOWS by Beverly Schappach, based on traditional block patterns, "Granny's Garden" and "Dresden Plate."

compatible with those for the top piece.

Next, with wrong sides facing, pin the quilted pillow top to the back fabric. Sew these pieces together, leaving a small opening in the top for turning. Never clip the excess from the corners of the pillows before turning, because this extra fabric helps the pillow look fuller. Turn the pillow inside out, stuff it and then sew the opening with a blind stitch.

Do you dislike working small? Do you prefer getting into the thick of the action?

Feel free to go on to larger projects. The principles are really the same.

Quilting With Blocks: Patchwork and Applique

Create a quilt made up of a series of blocks. Each block is first constructed as a single unit like the potholder. Then all the blocks are pieced together to form the entire quilt top.

CREATING IN CLOTH

For applique blocks, it is easiest to work on the same size blocks throughout. If you are going to repeat the same applique design in all or some of the blocks, you will have to create a template. If not, you may just cut freely from a sketch.

There are many applique quilts in which the block units are of different sizes. This is quite effective if planned carefully.

Planning the Whole

With all block quilting, first decide on the size of each block. This should be determined by your design. Some patterns lend themselves more readily to one size than another. You will have to judge which works best.

At the same time you are planning your block unit, you will need to have a sense of the total piece. Make a colored sketch on

Detail from PUTNAM COUNTY BICENTENNIAL QUILT, drawing of the DeWitt Clinton House by Gladys Boalt, finished piece executed by Betty Hatfield. Gladys Boalt © 1976.

graph paper in which the total number of squares represent the whole dimension of the quilt. Then designate a certain amount of little squares within the overall as being equal to one block unit. If you are going to add lattice strips, the narrow lengths of fabric which border and frame the block, you will need to draw them in also. This gives you a chart of the finished quilt: the total number of blocks and their size and placement, the size and placement of the border and the lattice strips (if you wish to use them) and the approximate color of every element of your quilt.

General quilt dimensions are as follows:

crib 40" × 60"
twin 72" × 90"
double 84" × 90"
queen 90" × 95"
king 102" × 100"

From your chart you can approximate how much fabric you will need to buy. The amount of fabric needed depends upon the kind of quilt you will make.

If you are making an applique quilt, you will have to guess at the amount of fabric you need for the applique pieces. You could decide on what the proportion of each color is to the quilt size and approximate how much fabric you need. For example, if you are making a baby quilt and green is used through half of the quilt, you can figure on getting one yard of green fabric 54" wide. Do not be afraid of buying too much. Then you will not run out of material even if you make a mistake, and you will have material left over for your scrap bag. Coordinate all your materials so that they are of similar weights and require the same kind of laundering or dry cleaning.

You can figure the yardage of a crazy quilt in the same way: ascertain the size of the top piece and then determine the proportion of colors and patterns you will need. Of course, for this kind of a project you can use all kinds of wonderful scraps. The Victorians were fond of satins and silks for their crazy quilts. Experiment with fabrics. Just make sure the materials are compatible and not too worn.

Determining yardage for a patchwork top is a bit more complicated. Using your graph

paper design, look at one block. Make a notation as to the size of each individual fabric color you have in that block. Multiply the size of each fabric color by the number of quilt blocks and you will arrive at the total amount of the fabric you will need for that color in the quilt top. Decide how many blocks will go into the width of your fabric, which probably will be somewhere between 36″ to 54″ wide. Do not forget to add the seam allowance and make sure you plan to cut all pieces with the grain going in the same direction. Keep a clear record showing each shape and color and the total amount of fabric needed for that piece in the quilt. Do the same kind of measuring and figuring for any lattice strips or borders.

You will have no trouble determining the size of the filler which will be the same size as the finished quilt. This is also true for the size of the backing, but only if you are going to finish your quilt by edging it with ready-made blanket binding. If you are going to bring the bottom up over the top edges or are going to turn both bottom and top edges in and hem them together, you will need to add at least 2″ more all the way around.

Putting the Blocks Together

When you put all the blocks together, you are faced with a number of possibilities.

The simplest method is to sew the blocks to each other in horizontal rows the width of the quilt. After pressing the seams to one side, each horizontal row is sewn to the next with one long seam which is pressed flat again. Later when the border is attached, the top will be ready for quilting.

Other possibilities are to place a plain block between two patchwork or applique blocks or to separate the rows of patchwork blocks with rows of lattice strips. Sew the blocks together in vertical rows the length of the quilt. Press the seams to one side. Sew the vertical rows to the lattice strips. Attach the border as described before and the piece is ready for quilting.

After your quilt top is finished, you will be able to mark the quilting design and then assemble the quilt "sandwich."

CREATING IN CLOTH

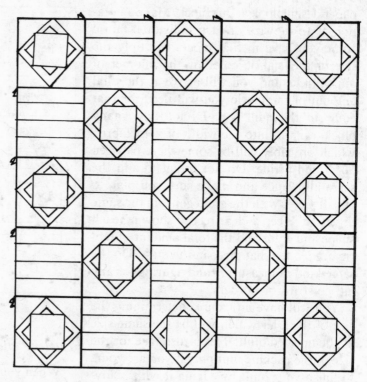

Examples of geometric and traditional schoolhouse designs.

Detail showing quilting around the coach from the PUTNAM COUNTY BICENTENNIAL QUILT. Gladys Boalt © 1976.

CREATING IN CLOTH

Block by Block Quilting

There is another technique for creating and assembling quilt blocks. With this method, each block is treated as if it were a tiny quilt. It is convenient to work this way. You do not need to bend over a frame to quilt. Everything is portable. You can take the little blocks with you and quilt them anywhere.

Begin by creating the top for each block in the same way other quilt blocks are assembled.

When all the blocks have been quilted, they are joined together in vertical strips by first stitching together the top layers of the blocks, right sides facing. Make sure to keep the batting and backing from catching in the seams. The strips are then sewn to each other in the same way by attaching the top layers. When this is completed, turn the quilt over and stitch together the edges of the backing by hand.

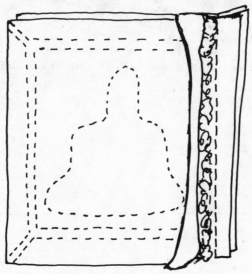

Finishing the Borders

Quilts look best with a border. It frames the piece, encloses it, sets it off as something special, and gives it a finished look. There are several ways of creating a border.

You can buy ready-made blanket binding to finish the edge of your quilt. With a running stitch (by machine) or a backstitch (by hand), attach the front of the binding to the front of the quilt.

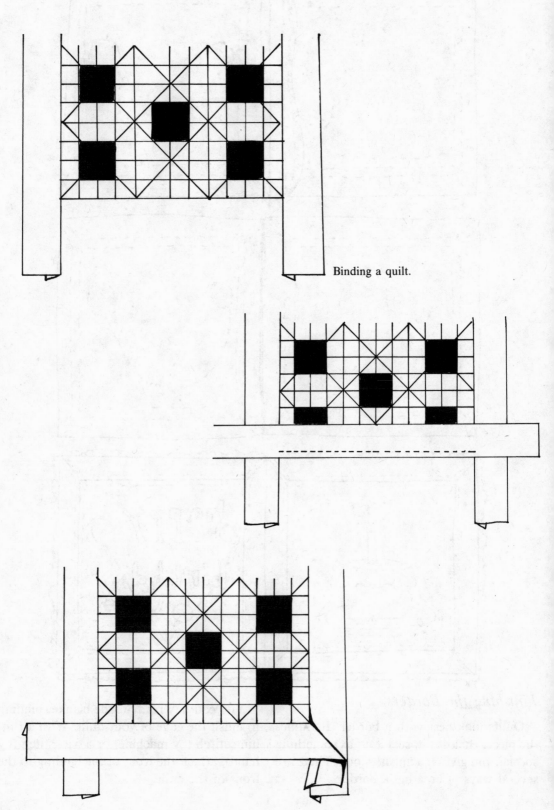

Binding a quilt.

for binding (finishing quilt)
1½ in bias strips
takes 1 yd. for straight edge (not scalloped)

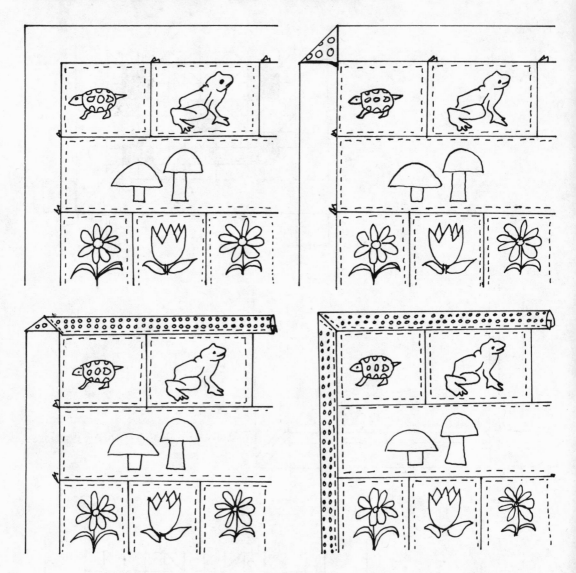

When the binding has been attached to all four sides, fold it over and sew it to the back with a blind stitch.

To finish by using the backing fabric as the border, turn the overlapping edge of the bottom layer over the top layer and hem it with a blind stitch as with the pot holder.

You can also finish your quilt by using the top fabric. Turn the edges over the backing and hem them with a blind stitch.

You now have a handsome quilt for warmth and display.

If you have skimmed through this chapter looking for ideas, but are not yet sure which project to undertake, consider looking ahead to the Soft Sculpture chapter. Remember that techniques for quilting are adaptable to all kinds of projects.

6. Soft Objects

CREATING IN CLOTH

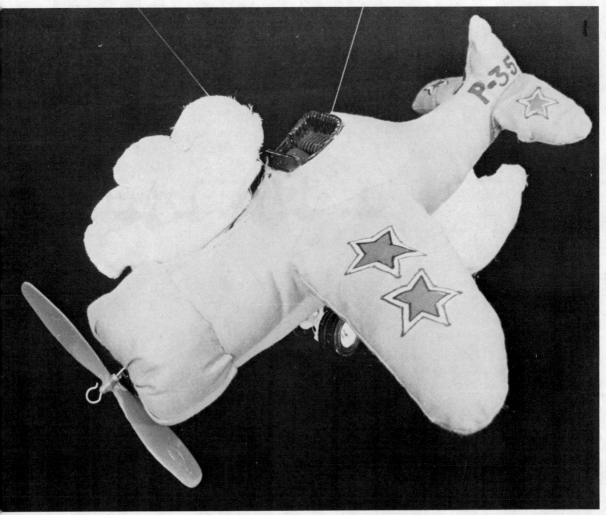

AIRPLANE, soft sculpture by Ellen Lyons.

Soft Objects

Years of teaching others have taught me that subject matter for soft sculpture is unlimited. In some of my classes, children have made lamps, boxes, airplanes, witches, bats, dragons, spaceships, telephones, clowns, animals and innumerable other three dimensional objects. Adults have made portraits of themselves or their families, cars, religious figures and butterflies.

Getting Started

You might think it easier to begin with a simple one-shape object and then go on to more complicated constructions; but it does not seem to work that way. Most people prefer to start with the object in mind and then learn the technique. Since I tend to work that way myself, I want to encourage you to do the same. Do not be bound to something in which you are not very interested just because it seems to be simplest. This is a stifling way to work. Instead, use your imagination. Do not set limits. Consider everything a possibility. And while you are dreaming about a project, read through this chapter to discover how to give your idea form.

What will the object be? Where will it be used and by whom? Is it for a boy or a girl? Is it decorative, for a couch or the floor, or

DOLL, by Jenny Ann Kalina, age eight, as a birthday present for her friend Julie Gearan.

CREATING IN CLOTH

will it hang on the wall? How big should it be? What fabrics should you use? What colors?

Begin to doodle. The first step is to make small drawings so that you have a concrete picture from which to work.

Basically, all stuffed objects are constructed in a similar way. Fabric is sewn together to form a pocket for the stuffing. Then the object is turned right side out, stuffed, and sewn together. The simplest construction is a one-shape doll since it requires only a front and a back.

Making Patterns

After you have made some sketches, draw the shape of the object in its finished size onto a large sheet of paper. Then add at least an extra inch all around. By the time the piece is sewn and stuffed it will have become much smaller. This is especially crucial where fingers or other slim shapes are used, because if their dimensions are too narrow, it is very difficult to turn them right side out.

When working with children, make it a point to have them draw a generous seam line all around their original sketch. Children find it difficult to understand this concept unless it is demonstrated to them so that they can see how much is lost in the seaming and turning.

Of course, if children are working in felt, there are no raw edges to turn. They can sew the edges of the object with the right sides facing out. They can even draw their design directly onto the felt. Using felt markers they can draw the shape, cut along the outlines, stitch and stuff and decorate quickly.

Choosing and Cutting the Cloth

Once a sketch has been made and cut from paper, it instantly becomes a pattern. With this pattern in hand, select a suitable fabric. For soft objects it is more practical to use washable fabrics and, as in quilt making, you should wash and iron them before beginning the object. Cotton, linen, velveteen, and other light to medium weight fabrics are the best choices.

Lay out two pieces of fabric, right sides together, on a flat surface. Usually you should match the pieces of fabric by cutting them so that the grain runs in the same direction on both pieces. However, there may be

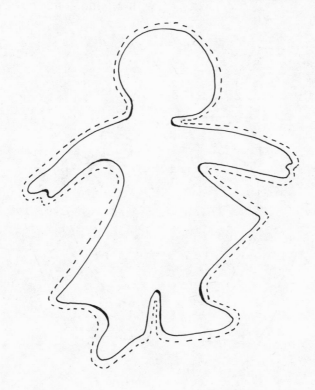

a reason you wish a piece to curl. In that case, cut it on the bias, diagonal to the grain. When a fabric is cut on the bias it stretches. You can discover bias by pulling the fabric in different directions.

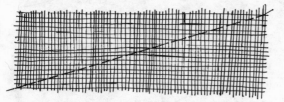

Cut out the fabric pieces by pinning the pattern to them and using it as a cutting guide. Take away the pattern and if you are not quilting or painting any pieces, pin the edges of the fabric (right sides still facing) and seam them together leaving a large enough opening so the piece can be turned right side out and stuffed. Clip the edges and turn the fabric.

Be patient if you are having trouble turning narrow shapes. These usually require extra effort and much pushing and pulling. Use either the eraser edge of a pencil, the wooden end of a narrow paint brush, a knitting needle or any appropriate tool. You will find these tools helpful for stuffing also, particularly in hard to reach or very slim areas.

Stuffing

Stuffing is easy. Work with small pieces of filler (see p. 39), one small bunch at a time. Make sure to get into every corner; leave no empty pockets. Children, especially, love to grab big bunches of stuffing and cram them in, but if you can encourage them to work patiently, the extra effort will prove to be well worth it.

After stuffing is completed, close the seam with a blind stitch.

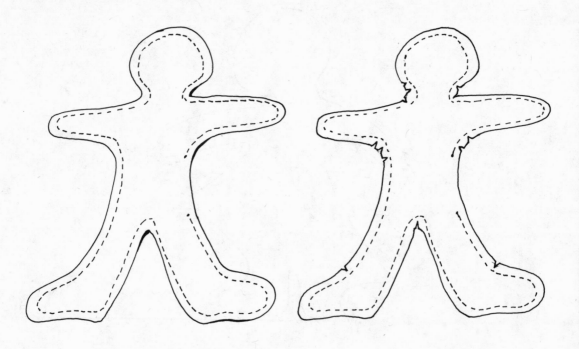

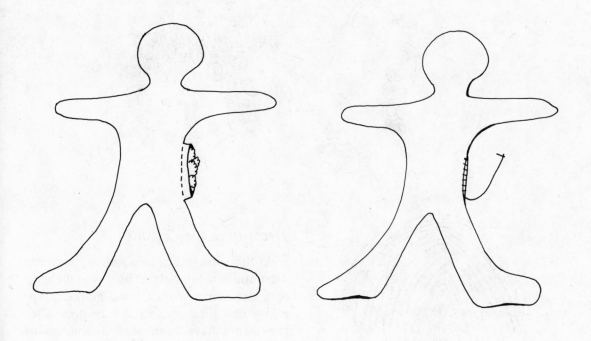

CREATING IN CLOTH

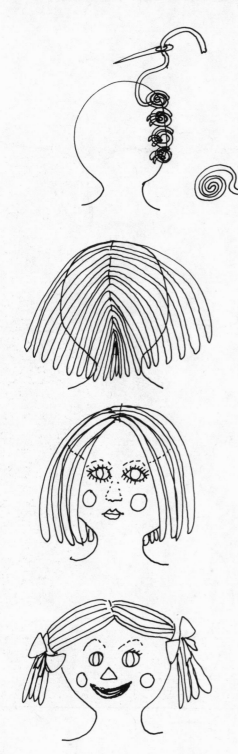

Decorating the Outside

At this time you can also add appropriate decorations to your object by using stitchery, applique, paints or waterproof markers. Applique and stitchery can also be done after the forms have been stuffed and seams closed.

If you plan to dye or quilt some parts or all of your work, you must do so after the original shape is cut from the fabric, but before the fabric pieces are sewn together. As in quilting, cut a third piece of lightweight cotton or muslin in the same shape as the outer pieces. Place batting between the cotton or muslin and the fabric, and the whole piece can be quilted. You can also quilt the surface of the soft sculpture with the trapunto technique described in the banner making chapter.

If you have made a doll and want to make clothes for it, use your doll as a guide. Draw a clothing pattern out of paper, giving yourself a seam allowance of at least one-half inch. Pin the paper pattern to the doll to make sure it will fit and is easily removable. The rest of the procedure is similar to making the doll itself. Place the pattern on two pieces of fabric which have their right sides facing, cut the fabric along the pattern outline, then seam and turn the article of clothing right sides out. Hem any raw edges. Pockets, buttons, snaps and bells, and all kinds of trimmings are appropriate final additions.

POSEIDON, soft object created by the author.

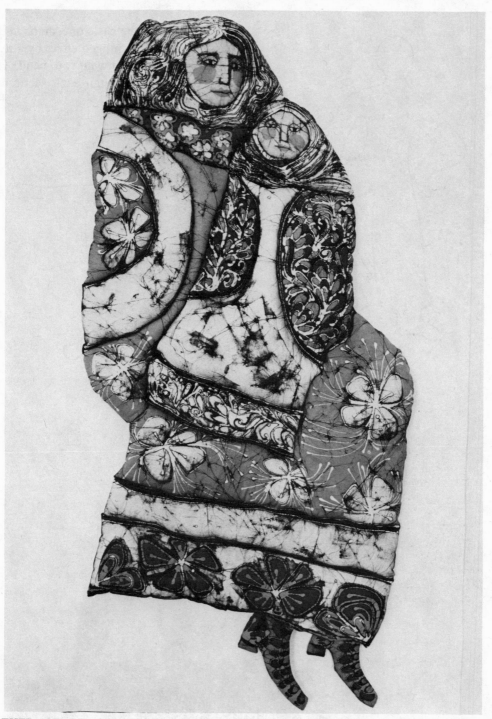

MOTHER AND CHILD, soft sculpture, quilted batik on muslin by Morag Benepe. From the collection of Carolyn Fabricant.

CREATING IN CLOTH

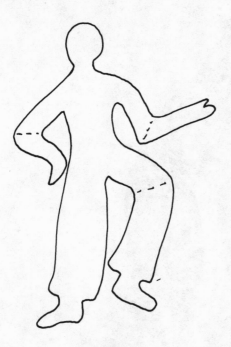

You can take the basic one-shape unit and create a jointed or hinged effect by stitching the places where you want it to bend. This is done by sewing through each section after you have stuffed it.

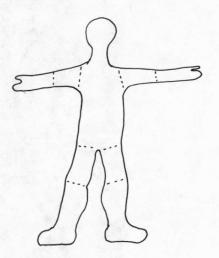

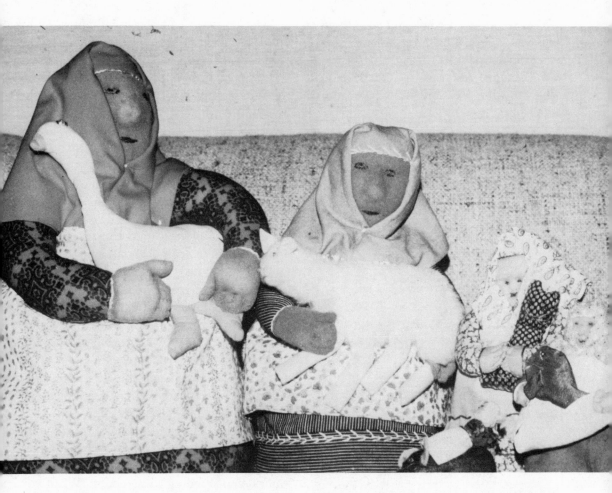

By adding extra forms onto the one-shape object, it is also possible to expand upon its original basic shape without getting into complicated constructions. All you have to do is to create other simple one-shape units and attach them to the main form. Think of this as building on, piece by piece. Sometimes such additions can be planned initially, as in the creation of a mother and child; other times, it may be fun to let your imagination go and just add on for the fun of it.

DOLLS, by Liese Bronfenbrenner.

CREATING IN CLOTH

Gussets are used when you wish to go beyond one-dimensional forms to more complicated constructions. Usually gussets are wedge-shaped and used to expand the lower edge outwards, so that the entire form can stand upright.

Many times a soft object will not stand by itself, even with the use of a gusset. Then you can add weights such as sand to assure proper balance. With smaller forms the insertion of a piece of thick cardboard in the bottom, before the stuffing has been added, will do the job.

One-shape soft objects can be made with or without a pattern, but when you design complicated forms with a front, back and sides or with a number of extensions, it is necessary to have a pattern. The easiest way to make the pattern is to construct a three dimensional paper model of the piece. This is not a difficult task and will save you hours of work. Not only can a paper model serve as a pattern, but it will also be a guide. Looking at it will help you visualize the final piece, make improvements, and decide if the project is worth undertaking.

Sketch as much information as you will need, such as where sections are joined and their proportions. Using this sketch as your guide, make a larger drawing of the different parts of the piece. Cut out these paper pieces and tape them together to form a three dimensional standing construction. When you are satisfied with the standing construction, mark the places where pieces should be seamed, and how many of each cut, then separate them so they become flat patterns again. Lay them on single or double fabric depending upon how many pieces of each you will need. Then, adding at least a one inch seam allowance, cut the shapes from the cloth. With a pencil, duplicate the markings you made on the paper on fabric. Then construct the paper model again so you will have a guide for the fabric construction. Always keep it in front of you for reference.

Your next step will be to duplicate the

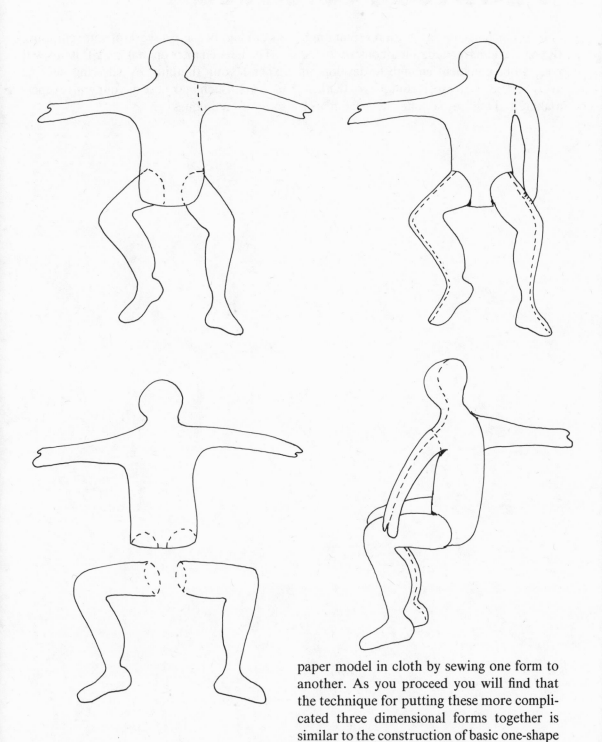

paper model in cloth by sewing one form to another. As you proceed you will find that the technique for putting these more complicated three dimensional forms together is similar to the construction of basic one-shape forms.

CREATING IN CLOTH

Creating soft objects requires planning. But once you have made a few constructions, you will be confident enough to develop an array of objects, to mix techniques of banner-making and quilting so that even a banner or a quilt can become a work of soft sculpture.

The next chapter on making gift items will expand your thinking by showing specific projects which make use of your entire repertoire of techniques.

7. Just for Giving

BABY QUILT, made by the staff and friends at Matthew Peterson Elementary School in Patterson for Jo Anne Tritto, an expectant mother. Each person made a square and participated in the quilting.

102

Just for Giving

This chapter shows the happy results of everything that has been discussed so far. Earlier chapters are technique-oriented, but this one will devote itself to presenting a gallery of ideas in finished form. From the assortment of gifts and decorations, you should be able to design your own projects for Christmas or for other holiday or gift-giving occasions.

At their own level, children can construct anything adults can make. Encouraging them to make a present instead of buying one instills in them a feeling for the greater meaning of gift-giving. Children love to create things. Allowing them to share their creations with others gives them a sense of confidence. They know you believe they do things well. It means much to them.

From cloth, children can create dolls, stuffed animals, Christmas stockings, beanbags and banners. They can create bookmarks, eyeglass cases, and bookcovers.

Teach them how to sew by hand and by machine when they are of an appropriate age.

Detail from CELEBRATIONS, a group banner created in a federally funded workshop, led by the author at the Mark Twain Jr. High School for the Gifted and Talented in Brooklyn.

CREATING IN CLOTH

Seasonal Banners

Begin with a banner or hanging. Banners are wonderfully festive. A Christmas banner can express anything from the special joy of welcoming friends and family to something of the deepest religious significance. Using words and symbols, you can extend a personal message or a group message. Work alone or let the activity of banner making be a celebration which includes your family, your friends, or your class. Work on one large banner together or string up a row of individual banners. Use felt if you want to work quickly and boldly or use other materials suggested in chapter three. Add festive decorations. Decide whether you will use your banner

ECCE HOMO BANNER designed and made by Lois James after drawings in GOOD NEWS FOR MODERN MAN

year round or will display it only at this holiday time.

Banners With Pockets

For a very young child, banners can be made with pockets for storing soft toys which you have made.

The same idea on a more sophisticated level can become a handy wall-organizer.

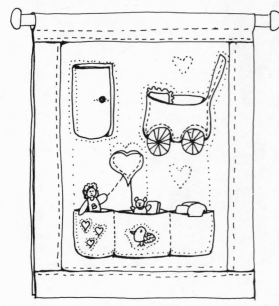

Pocket banner for a child.

Pocket banner for an adult.

CREATING IN CLOTH

Pocketbook

Need a banner always hang on a wall? Does a quilt have to function as a bed covering? Why not reduce the elements to a smaller size to create the pot holder or pillow discussed at the beginning of chapter 5? You can also add some handles, and give a friend, a child or parent a handmade applique or quilted pocketbook.

TOTE BAGS by Carol Leonard.

BABY QUILT AND TOTE BAG, based on traditional quilt designs, by Nicki Huebbe.

Plan the shape, size and construction of your bag before designing the applique or patchwork which will decorate it. The most basic bag consists of a front and a back piece. Without handles it will look like a soft envelope; with handles it can be anything from a tote bag to an everyday pocketbook.

Cut your pattern pieces from newsprint paper in the size you wish the finished bag. Tape the pieces together. If the proportions are correct, you now have a working pattern.

You will find this pattern-making procedure similar to the soft sculpture procedure (p. 88) except that you will not stuff the inside of the object.

On your paper construct, use a felt marker to note where seams meet. Carefully take the pieces apart, lay them on the fabric, pin them, and add a seam allowance. Check to see that the grain or pattern runs in a consistent direction for each piece. Then cut the pieces from the fabric. Re-assemble your paper pattern for easy reference.

CREATING IN CLOTH

Add decorations to the fabric pieces before you assemble them. Any technique from applique to patchwork, from stitchery to trapunto is appropriate.

To make a fabric handle, you need to measure the length it will be plus the seam allowance. Fold a long piece of fabric in half with the right sides together. Cut the strip, pin it closed, seam it, turn it right side out and attach it to the bag.

Some fabrics are too thick to turn right side out. In this case, cut a wide strip and fold it over, one edge overlapping the other. Turn under the raw edge and blindstitch it closed.

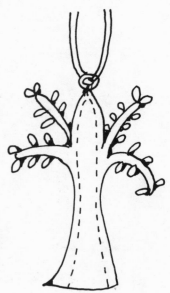

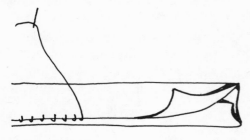

Neckpieces

Consider creating a miniature stuffed banner to be worn around the neck. Neckpieces made from cloth are attractive and lightweight. They make beautiful, highly original gifts for children or special friends.

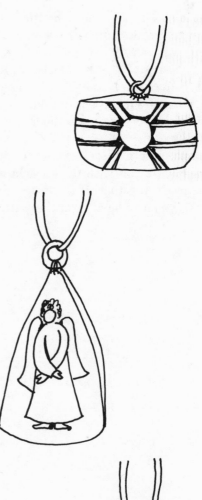

108

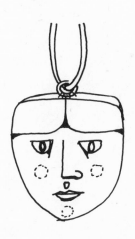
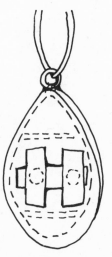

Cut two pieces of fabric, and decorate the front of the neckpiece. With the right sides together, sew the seams leaving an opening. Turn the neckpiece right side out, stuff it, and sew the opening closed. Sew a small bead or a loop on the top and thread it with a leather thong or a ribbon.

Pillows

Applique and embroider your family tree or your home onto a pillow or banner. It is a gift suitable for young and old alike, a wonderful personal remembrance, a future heirloom.

Detail from BABY QUILT, by staff and friends at Matthew Peterson Elementary School in Patterson.

CREATING IN CLOTH

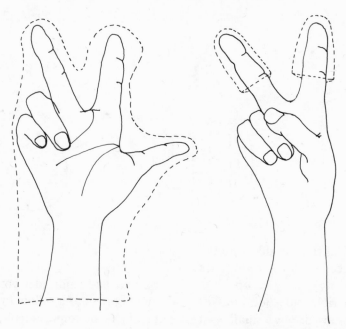

Puppets

Hand and finger puppets are as easy to make as soft toys and pillows. For the basic form, you will need two pieces of cloth for the front and the back. These are sewn together to create a pocket for a hand or finger.

Make a paper pattern first. Place it over two pieces of fabric, right sides together. Making sure to include a seam allowance, cut out the two pieces. Before you sew them together, decorate the front with any of the techniques described in the preceding chapters.

Soft Book

Consider making a soft book. Develop a theme and create some drawings or collages. Decide on the page size.

the pages back to back, turn in the edges and hem. Create a spine by sewing a seam up the center.

Soft Box

Create a soft box from cloth and cardboard. Luxurious textures and decorations can make it into a beautiful gift for storing treasured items.

Squares and rectangles are easy to use in the construction of a soft box. Think of each side as if it were a stuffed pillow with a piece

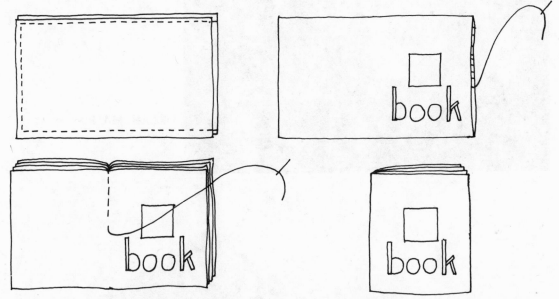

Out of paper, cut double sized pages and fold them over to see if the proportion is suitable. Place the paper on fabric and cut out twice the amount of pages for the book. (Placing the pages back to back will give them more weight.)

Choose a sturdy fabric for the cover.

Decorate the front side of each page with objects a child enjoys naming. When you are finished stitching or gluing them on, place

of cardboard for support. You will need six pieces of sturdy cardboard and twelve pieces of fabric. The fabric should be cut one inch larger than the cardboard for the seam allowance and the stuffing.

After the fabric has been cut, decorate any of the outsides you want to embellish. Stitching, appliqueing, painting and quilting are all possibilities. However, if you are going to add heavy trimmings, such as bells, beads, mirrors, and other non-fabric materials, do

CREATING IN CLOTH

OKLAHOMA BOX by Wilna Lane.

EMBROIDERED BOX
by Hannelore Soderstrom.

not place them on the box until it has been assembled.

With the decorating finished, the two pieces are sewn together like pillows. With right sides facing, seam the two pieces of fabric, leaving one complete side open, turn inside out, insert the cardboard, stuff tightly with filler, and close with a slip stitch. Do this for all six pairs, but do not stuff the inside of the top cover or it will not close properly.

To build the box, attach the six sides to each other with a blind stitch.

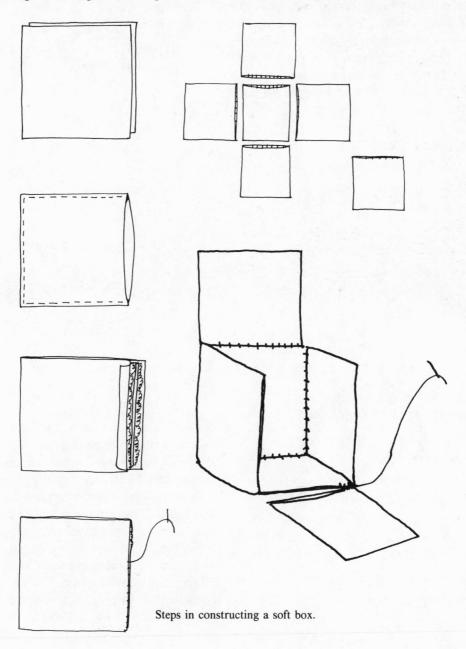

Steps in constructing a soft box.

CREATING IN CLOTH

Masks

Although they may seem most appropriate for Halloween or birthday parties, I think masks are enjoyable anytime. Any adult or child who can create a mask from paper or cardboard can easily create one from the more durable cloth.

Very young children often make their masks from paper plates. They cut holes for eyes and draw or glue on decorations, including hair. The same can be done with a piece

of felt. Fortify the holes with curtain rings and tie a ribbon to each side. Fasten behind the head, and a mask has been made.

An older child can create a three-dimensional mask to cover the entire head, front and back. A pattern can be made from separate pieces of paper taped together or from a paper bag which has been cut apart to serve as a pattern. Remember to allow for seams when cutting from cloth. The concept and construction is similar to that of soft toys and pillows.

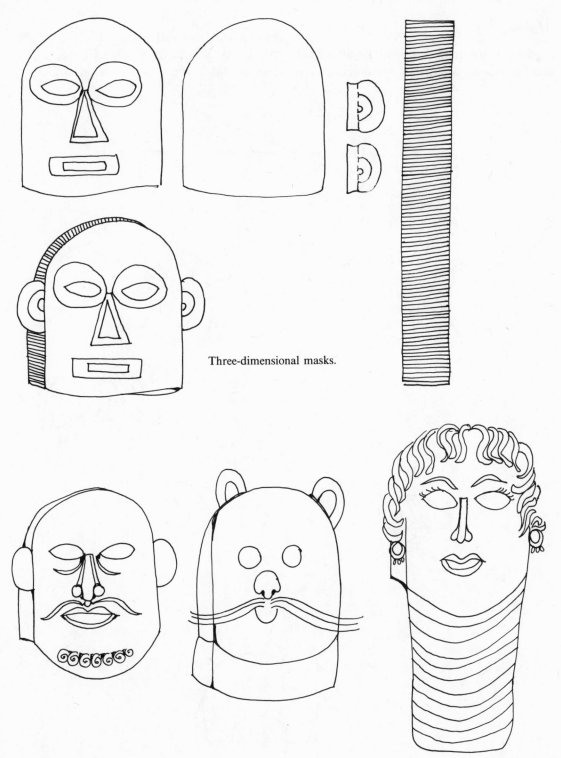

Three-dimensional masks.

CREATING IN CLOTH

Mobiles

Mobiles are great fun to make, beautiful, and fascinating when they are finished. The easiest way to construct a mobile is to suspend soft objects from a large ring, a coat hanger, thick wires or a wooden dowel.

MOTHER AND DAUGHTER ANGEL, patterns and finished dolls made by Nora Kalina at age seven.

Dolls or Animals

An obvious and favored gift for a youngster is a stuffed doll or stuffed animal. Children may have many toys, but they always prefer these soft objects. They treasure their rag dolls and lop-eared elephants. They sleep with their arms around them and play with them for hours. The Soft Sculpture chapter illustrates construction and designing techniques.

CREATING IN CLOTH

CHESS PIECES by Liese Bronfenbrenner.

Soft Games

Another gift you can make for a child or an adult is a game made from fabric, such as a stuffed checker board and checkers or a quilted beanbag toss game, which can be played with on the floor and then hung on the wall like a banner for display.

Stuffed Tree Ornaments

Lovely Christmas tree ornaments can be made of cloth. Try to envision your tree hung with stuffed forms this year. Angels, the Holy Family, the magi, the shepherds, tiny toys, Christmas stockings—all and more can be stuffed and suspended from the tree.

Small objects, however, are difficult to turn right side out. One way to avoid this problem is to use felt for all your pieces. But there is such a wonderful range of fabrics available to you that there is no reason to limit yourself. You can create soft objects without turning the raw edge. Simply cut your fabrics right sides out and sew them together that way by edging with the zigzag stitch, leaving an opening to push in the stuffing. Then sew it closed with the zigzag, and trim the edges close to the stitching. Thread a needle with yarn, pull it through the top, make a loop, tie it off with a bow and you have a stuffed Christmas tree ornament.

STUFFED CHRISTMAS TREE ORNAMENTS by Ellen Lyons.

CREATING IN CLOTH

Stuffed Creche

Why not try to create a creche? From the Soft Sculpture chapter, you already know how to create a stuffed form. You can apply this knowledge to make a group of figures. The relationship between the figures will be important: coordinating colors, keeping them a similar size, and making them a part of the grouping will be your main concerns.

Begin by making a sketch of the group, and then go on to drawing a pattern for each piece. You will probably want each figure to stand, so each will require a gusset. To insure proper balance, do not forget to place cardboard and/or sand inside each figure.

Creating the creche can be as simple or as complex as you like. Figures can all be of the

STUFFED CRECHE created by the author.

CREATING IN CLOTH

same size and shape made from only one pattern, or they can be of varying sizes and shapes, so that you will need a separate pattern for each soft piece.

Here, as in earlier projects, there is no need to limit yourself to only a few materials or techniques. Decorations can be stitched or created with markers, paints or dyes. Trimmings from ribbons to bells can be added.

There is no limit to the projects you can devise and adapt to different individual needs, age groups and abilities. This book is only a beginning for you. Go on from here and, in the future, think of it as a resource. Turn to it for ideas, for technical information and for inspiration.

GOOD LUCK!

FOR YOUR CREATIVE DESIGNS.